Beauty
and the Beast

A PLAY FOR CHILDREN

By Nicholas Stuart Gray

No part of this book may be reproduced, stored in a retrieval system, or transmitted in any form, by any means, including mechanical, electronic, photocopying, recording, or otherwise, without the prior written permission of the publisher.

SAMUEL FRENCH, INC.
25 WEST 45TH STREET   NEW YORK 10036
7623 SUNSET BOULEVARD   HOLLYWOOD 90046
LONDON   *TORONTO*

COPYRIGHT ©, 1951, BY NICHOLAS STUART GRAY

ALL RIGHTS RESERVED

CAUTION: Professionals and amateurs are hereby warned that BEAUTY AND THE BEAST is subject to a royalty. It is fully protected under the copyright laws of the United States of America, the British Commonwealth, including Canada, and all other countries of the Copyright Union. All rights, including professional, amateur, motion pictures, recitation, lecturing, public reading, radio broadcasting, television and the rights of translation into foreign languages are strictly reserved. In its present form the play is dedicated to the reading public only.

BEAUTY AND THE BEAST may be given stage presentation by amateurs upon payment of a royalty of Fifteen Dollars for each performance, payable one week before the date when the play is given, to Samuel French, Inc., at 25 West 45th Street, New York, N. Y. 10036, or at 7623 Sunset Boulevard, Hollywood, Calif. 90046, or to Samuel French (Canada), Ltd., 80 Richmond Street East, Toronto, Ontario, Canada M5C 1P1.

Royalty of the required amount must be paid whether the play is presented for charity or gain and whether or not admission is charged.

Stock royalty quoted on application to Samuel French, Inc.

For all other rights than those stipulated above, apply to Ms. Joan Ling, c/o English Theatre Guild Ltd., 1, The Pavement, London, SW4 OHY, England.

Particular emphasis is laid on the question of amateur or professional readings, permission and terms for which must be secured in writing from Samuel French, Inc.

Copying from this book in whole or in part is strictly forbidden by law, and the right of performance is not transferable.

Whenever the play is produced the following notice must appear on all programs, printing and advertising for the play: "Produced by special arrangement with Samuel French, Inc."

Due authorship credit must be given on all programs, printing and advertising for the play.

Anyone presenting the play shall not commit or authorize any act or omission by which the copyright of the play or the right to copyright same may be impaired.

No changes shall be made in the play for the purpose of your production unless authorized in writing.

The publication of this play does not imply that it is necessarily available for performance by amateurs or professionals. Amateurs and professionals considering a production are strongly advised in their own interests to apply to Samuel French, Inc., for consent before starting rehearsals, advertising, or booking a theatre or hall.

Printed in U.S.A.

ISBN 0 573 65008 X

TO LENORE, MY MOTHER,
   with love

AUTHOR'S NOTE

There is a good deal of real hard magic in this play. And it takes thousands of years to get all the spells right.

However, in case you should want to act the play, I've worked out some simpler ways of making roses droop and eggs light up, and other unlikely things. You may like to experiment for yourselves to produce these effects. But, if your time and your magic run short, write to the Oxford University Press, telling them where and when you wish to produce the play, and they will send you a list of easy instructions.

At least, I hope you will find them easy. Magic is preferable—if you happen to have five thousand years to spare.

Act One   *Scene One*

THE WIZARD'S BACK GARDEN

The WIZARD *has made his back garden in a little clearing in a forest. All round it crouch the dark trees. The things he grows in it are not quite usual.*

The roof and gables of the WIZARD'S *cottage can be seen at a little distance, with a curious contraption running up to the chimney, rather like a storm-cone.*

It is twilight, and the moon is shining with increasing brilliance as the night deepens. Out among the garden bushes, from a lower window in the cottage, shines a soft candle-light.

The WIZARD *comes down the garden path, among the unlikely plants and trees. He is a small, round, charming-looking old gentleman, wearing a long robe, and a conical cap. He is earnestly banging a little brass gong.*

WIZARD. Mikey ! Mikey ! Dinner's ready. [*He bangs the gong again, peering among the trees.*] Mikey ! Oh, dear me, it *is* getting so late, and I don't like the child to be out in the forest after dark. Mikey ! Dinner ! [*He crosses the stage, banging the gong. There is a wild outburst of cock-crowing from under a great tree, and the* WIZARD *jumps backwards.*] Oh, my dear goodness gracious ! Oh, my hat and my nerves ! I've been and trodden on Cocky-olly. Poor old boy, then. There, there. . . . Come to silly old clumsy Hodge, then. Come on. Where are you ? I can't see you in the shadow. [*He stoops into the darkness behind the tree, and then comes back into the moonlight, with a large black cock clinging on to his shoulder.*] Poor old Cocky-olly. We did frighten each other, didn't we ? I went and trod right on your lovely nest with my silly big foot. And there you were, so busy thinking out how to lay me a magic egg. All the other cock birds eat their magic eggs, but you won't . . . now will you ? You're a much cleverer cock-bird than the others, because you belong to me and I'm a wizard. You will keep on trying, won't you, dear ? If you lay me a beautiful black egg, I can make spells that have never come off properly before. If I had that egg now, for instance, I could make a spell that would bring my little nephew home right away, out of the dark and the nasty forest. But there, I'm not trying to rush you, Cocky dear. You do it in your own time, but do keep on thinking about it. Mikey ! Come to dinner ! Mikey ! [*He bangs the gong again, and the* COCK *crows.*] My gracious ! Not right in my ear ! Now, listen, was that someone calling ? Is that Mikey ?

MIKEY [*off*]. Here I come, Uncle Hodge.

WIZARD. About time, too. Your dinner's getting cold.

[*Enter* MIKEY. *He is a baby dragon. Rather plump, and very little, with scales, and a ridge of spikes down his spine, from his round head to his pointed tail that just touches the ground behind him. He walks, or rather bounds energetically on his hind legs.*]

MIKEY. I'm sorry, Uncle Hodge.

WIZARD. You're a naughty little dragon. I'll tell your mother. Where have you been? The forest is a most uncertain place to be alone in, after the light goes.

MIKEY. I like it in the moonlight, Uncle.

WIZARD. But it isn't safe. My goodness gracious me, you silly little dragon, you've no idea what sort of things can happen in a forest so full of magic as this one.

MIKEY. You're not afraid of magic, are you, Uncle Hodge? You're a magician.

WIZARD. Yes, yes, of course I am. A very good magician, on a modest scale. But there's things can happen in a forest that no average magician can do anything to avoid. Come along. The bread-and-milk are ready this half hour. There, Cocky-olly, I'd nearly forgotten and taken you into the cottage, and you don't care for bread-and-milk. You sit down again on your nice cosy nest, and go on thinking about laying an egg for me, there's a dear bird.

MIKEY. My mum says that when a black cock lays an egg, he does it at midnight, and then eats it.

WIZARD. I've spoken to Cocky very seriously about that, and we must just hope for the best.

[*He settles Cocky-olly comfortably down in the shadow of the tree. He says over his shoulder:*

WIZARD. Why were you so late, Mikey? I told you to come home by sunset.

MIKEY. I saw interesting things in the forest, and I sort of got slow.
WIZARD. Oh dear me, you shouldn't stop to look at things in a very magic forest. What did you see?
MIKEY. I saw a bat, and I saw a swan...
WIZARD. You could see those from my garden here, child.
MIKEY. I saw a blue owl.
WIZARD. There are lots in this forest.
MIKEY. And a great unicorn.
WIZARD. They come to my gate for sugar.
MIKEY. I saw a young man, riding fast on a white horse.
WIZARD. He shouldn't be in the forest after dark.
MIKEY. I saw an elephant.
WIZARD. You saw what?
MIKEY. An elephant ... with wings ... what flew.
  [*There is a distant crash on a deep gong, and a storm-cone rushes up the wire to the chimney of the cottage.*]
WIZARD [*appalled*]. Oh, Mikey, you've told a whacker.
MIKEY. I didn't.
WIZARD. You shouldn't say that. It'll do it again.
  [*And it does.*]
That was two whackers. Two real lies. Mikey, you are a very bad dragon.
MIKEY. I didn't know there was going to be bangs.
WIZARD. That's my lie-detector. I invented that after tea. If anyone tells a lie, and it hears, up goes the storm-cone, and an invisible gong sounds.
MIKEY. Oh.
WIZARD. Your mother warned me, when you came to stay after you had measles. She said you sometimes tell awful whackers. So I invented that. You bad dragon. Naughty Mikey.
MIKEY [*sniffing*]. Don't care.

WIZARD. Oh, you do.
> [*The storm-cone does it again.*]

You see. That was another whacker. You do care. Now, that's enough, Mikey. There, there, child. Just don't do it again.

MIKEY. I'll try not.

WIZARD. Good boy. It's so silly to say you see things that aren't really there. As if there aren't enough curious things to see that *are* there.

MIKEY. I can see a white horse, Uncle Hodge.

WIZARD. Mikey, you mustn't say that. It'll do it again.

MIKEY. But I can. A great white horse, galloping among the trees, over there.

WIZARD. Untruthful child ... unreliable dragon....

MIKEY. Well, it hasn't banged yet. Look, Uncle ... listen.
> [*A pause. The* WIZARD *looks at the storm-cone, then puts his head on one side to listen. Not very far away can be heard the thudding of a horse's hoofs on a grass path.*]

WIZARD. Dear me, I *am* sorry, Mikey. You were quite right.

MIKEY. I wonder if it's the young man I saw in the forest? Oh ... oh dear....

WIZARD. What's the matter?

MIKEY. I wonder if he's coming after me?

WIZARD. Why should he?

MIKEY. Oh, Uncle, I'm frightened. I was hiding in a bush and I saw the young man, and he shot a heron....

WIZARD. Dear me, what a pity ... they're so decorative.

MIKEY. So is he ... but Uncle, he looks so angry and wild. He has a scarlet cloak and tawny hair, and ... and I'm afraid of him.

WIZARD. Why?

MIKEY. Well, when he shot the heron, I hated him, so I made my mooing noise, you know the one?
WIZARD. My gracious, yes. Very disturbing.
MIKEY. And it frightened his horse, and it reared up and went racing away through the forest . . . and the young man was very angry. I wouldn't like to meet him.
WIZARD. Well, I'm afraid you're going to.
MIKEY. Yes, he's got off his horse at the gate. Uncle. . . .
WIZARD. Courage, child, he won't bite you.
MIKEY. I'm not so sure.

> [*He takes refuge behind his Uncle, and they watch the* PRINCE *come striding through the trees*, R. *He is breathless and angry, and in a hurry. His tawny hair falls untidily on his shoulders and his young face is arrogant, and sulky. A boy who is rough and rude, as the* WIZARD *can clearly see. He is also unhappy, which is not immediately apparent to the alarmed* HODGE.]

PRINCE [*breathlessly*]. Which is the way to the north?
WIZARD. Er . . . over there, sir. At least . . . my goodness, I'm nearly sure *that's* the south [*pointing*] . . . so the opposite. . . .
PRINCE. What are you babbling about? Can't you answer a simple question? All I want to know is . . . where I am, and which way to go.
WIZARD. You're in my garden, sir . . . standing on my best mandrake! And the way to the north is . . . over there . . . I think.

> [*He has now pointed in every direction of the compass, and the* PRINCE *shouts at him.*]

PRINCE. Stop waving your stupid arms! As for your mandrake . . . whatever that may be . . . [*He grinds his boot on the ground.*]

WIZARD. Oh, my goodness! How very naughty of you! I raised it from seed, and watered it every day.

MIKEY. Oh, you beast!

WIZARD. Mikey! Manners!

PRINCE [*rather startled*]. What's that? Your tame lizard?

MIKEY. I'm not a lizard! I'm not!

PRINCE [*bored with them both*]. Now come, you old fool! Will you tell me the way out of this forest, or must I force you to?

WIZARD. Now come, young man ... there's no call to be in so bad a temper.

PRINCE. Don't address me so, you peasant. You are speaking to a prince.

MIKEY. You don't behave like one.

WIZARD. Mikey ... manners. ...

PRINCE. I'll deal with the lizard later. Tell me the way to the north.

WIZARD. Er. ...

PRINCE. Or I'll stamp your wretched garden into mud.

[*He sets his boot on another plant and grinds it into the earth.*]

WIZARD. Oh my dear gracious goodness! The little sunflower!

MIKEY. Oh, you *are* a beast!

PRINCE. Are you speaking to me, lizard?

MIKEY. Yes. And I'm not a lizard. ... I'm a dragon.
[*The* PRINCE *laughs unkindly.*]

PRINCE. You little lying lizard. You're no dragon.

MIKEY. And you're no prince. ... You're a beast, that's what.

WIZARD. Mikey, manners! What would your mother say?

PRINCE. Enough of this. Old fool, come and point me out some track that will lead me home, before I lose my temper completely.

WIZARD [*quickly*]. Er... er... oh yes, sir.... I think I can show you a path leading... er... in a roughly northerly direction. Let me show you... you mustn't lose your temper.... I mean, my goodness, it's bad enough where it is.

PRINCE. Are you being insolent?

WIZARD Me? Oh dear, dear, don't say things like that in front of the child.... I wouldn't dream of being insolent, young man... your Highness... oh, do come along and I'll show you the path.

PRINCE I very seldom allow myself to lose my temper, let me tell you.

[*The storm-cone runs up, and the gong crashes.*]

MIKEY. He's told a whacker, Uncle.

PRINCE What was that?

WIZARD. That was my lie-detector, Prince. It... sort of goes off when it hears anyone tell a lie.

PRINCE. If you weren't so old and mad, I'd break your stupid neck... and squash your lizard with my boot.

MIKEY If I was a grown-up dragon, I'd bite you.

PRINCE [*shouting*]. Which is the way to the north?

WIZARD. Oh, come along... yes... you see, that's the North Star... no, that one... oh dear, is it?

PRINCE. If you think me a fit subject for your foolery, you must learn better I came here to hunt, and I've been lost since noon, and I've had enough of the forest and everything in it.

MIKEY. Well, go quick! Everything's had enough of you. You shot a beautiful heron.... I saw you, and I'm glad I mooed at you ... and I'm glad your horse ran away with you. ...

PRINCE. What's that?

MIKEY. I hate you.

WIZARD. Mikey, what would your mother. ...

MIKEY. You're a beastly ... beastly ... beast ... so there!

PRINCE. I'll put my foot on you, you lizard.

MIKEY. I'll bite you.

[*The PRINCE seizes him, and holds him fast for all his struggles.*]

PRINCE. Now, you old fool. Tell me the way to the north quickly.

WIZARD. I can't remember which is the right way, you've got me so confused with all this violence and temper.

PRINCE. I'll count five. And if you haven't remembered by then, I shall break the neck of this lizard, and set my foot on it.

WIZARD. Oh, my great goodness ... don't be so naughty!

PRINCE. One.

MIKEY. Let me go ... you beast! You beast!

WIZARD. This isn't good behaviour for a prince. Whatever would your mother say?

PRINCE. I haven't one. Two.

WIZARD. Your father, then?

PRINCE. I have none. I have neither relatives, nor friends. I live alone, in a great castle, with paid servants who fear me.

WIZARD. Well, really, can you blame them. You *are* rough.

PRINCE. Three.

WIZARD. What? Oh . . . oh, heavens! Do stop! Let my little nephew go. We've done you no harm, Prince. Oh dear, we want to help you . . . really. Why can't I think of any magic? I'm all rattled.

MIKEY. You're hurting me. . . . Don't. . . .

PRINCE. I'll hurt you more in a minute, lizard. Hurry up, old lunatic, and remember the way to the north. Four.

WIZARD. My hat and my aunt! Listen, I'll say a bit of magic. Something might happen . . . I might remember the North Star . . . and it's pretty, anyway.

PRINCE. You'd better hurry.

WIZARD. Weave a circle round him thrice,
Wish a wish, and think of mice.

PRINCE. Well?

WIZARD. That's all. Now I wish . . . magic, magic, do happen. Help!

> [*There is a loud crowing from* COCKY. *The* PRINCE *starts, and* MIKEY *bites him and escapes. He runs to the* WIZARD *and they both cower. The* PRINCE *puts his hand in his mouth and glares at them. Then he draws his sword.*]

Now, don't do that! Don't be so naughty!

PRINCE. I think I've lost my temper completely now, with the pair of you. You've asked for it.

> [COCKY-OLLY *crows again.*]

MIKEY. I wish my mum was here.

WIZARD. Oh! Oh, my goodness me! Look! [*He stoops and then holds out on his hand a big black egg.*] Cocky's done it! And it isn't even midnight, yet.

PRINCE. Don't try to distract me with a common egg.

WIZARD. It's no common egg, this one. It's magic. Listen to this:

>   Tail-less rats,
>   And wingless bats,
>   Earthworm's leg,
>   And Cocky's egg,
>   Magic be
>   For me.

> [*There is a green flash, and the sword falls from the* PRINCE'S *hand.*]

See?

> [*The* PRINCE *tries to move, but is unable to. He glares at the* WIZARD.]

PRINCE. You'll be sorry for this.

WIZARD. No, I'm afraid you will.

PRINCE. What's holding me?

WIZARD. Magic, young man The magic that you've been laughing at all this time.

PRINCE. Let me go.

WIZARD. Good gracious no, you're too wild, and rough.

MIKEY. He's a beast, Uncle.

WIZARD. Do you know, I'm afraid you're right. I'll have to take a very serious line with him ... there's no other way.

MIKEY. Can I bite him again?

WIZARD. Most certainly you may not.

PRINCE. Do you mean to keep me here in this forest all night?

WIZARD. I'm going to keep you here in the forest for twenty years, young man.

PRINCE. Are you mad? Do you think you can?

WIZARD. Yes...as a matter of fact, I do rather think I can.

PRINCE. Twenty years! You can't hold me here for another five minutes. And when I get at you, heaven help you.

MIKEY. Don't talk to my uncle like that. If he says you're going to stay here for another twenty years, well, you just are. He's a very good magician.

WIZARD. Well, average good.

PRINCE. He's a crazed old idiot! I'd like to see his magic.

WIZARD. You're feeling a bit of it now, young man.

PRINCE [*furiously*]. All right. What are you going to do next?

WIZARD. Now let me see. Well, next I think I'm going to invent a castle for you to live in. Yes, indeed, that's what I'll do next.

MIKEY. A castle, Uncle?

WIZARD. Well, he must live somewhere, mustn't he? And he is a prince, whatever his behaviour. I can't put him in a dog-kennel.

MIKEY. He'd look just right with a chain round his neck. We could put a notice on the garden gate, saying 'Beware of the Prince'.

WIZARD. Mikey, I will not have this rudeness. It's most undragonly to speak like that to someone who is not in a position to argue. Apologize.

MIKEY. Sorry. But not very.

WIZARD. You be careful, or I'll send you to the castle with him.

MIKEY. No... oh, no. I *am* sorry, now.

PRINCE. What castle? There is no castle here.

WIZARD. There's going to be in a minute, young man.

MIKEY. Here, Uncle? Oh no, not too near. It's so quiet and nice here, usually. It would be horrid and rough if he was anywhere about.

WIZARD. There's something in that, Mikey. I'd better put it some way off. About thirty miles away, I think.

Yes, there's a lovely thick patch of briars and beech trees that I know of. I'll put the castle right in the middle. [*reassuringly to the* PRINCE] It's pretty there.

PRINCE. Do you think I'd stay in it for longer than a minute?

WIZARD. I shall arrange that you can't get out.

PRINCE. You're going to imprison me?

WIZARD. Oh no, it won't be as bad as that, I promise you. After all, one castle is as good as another if there's no one that you like who lives in it with you.

PRINCE. Then what is the point?

WIZARD. As my nephew rather rudely told you, you're a beast. And beasts have to be taught good manners. I think that when you've been alone in a magic castle, you'll grow tired of being a beast, and you'll want to be a man again. Then I shall come and let you out. Do you understand?

PRINCE. I'd like to kill you.

WIZARD. You'll have to grow out of that.

PRINCE. Never. Even if you really can do this to me, I shall stay the same for twenty years, or fifty years, or a hundred years ... and I shall kill you at the end of it. Now get on with your stupid magic, and let's see what happens.

WIZARD. Very well. You can't say you haven't asked for it, you know.

[*He lifts the black egg up in the moonlight.*]

    All the forest magic lies
    Hidden safe from human eyes,
    Strong enchantment, mighty spells,
    Powerful necromancy dwells
    In the round and newly-laid
    Egg that Cocky-olly made.

[COCKY-OLLY *crows.*]

PRINCE. Is that all?

WIZARD. Not by many a long chalk. You just listen to this:

> Magic hid in Cocky's egg,
> Do my bidding now, I beg.

[*The egg is suddenly studded all over with bright stars.*]

MIKEY. Oooh.

WIZARD. Deep within the briar brake,
> Now a mighty castle make,
> Set with spells all round about
> That the Prince may not get out:
> Holding him with magic powers
> Safe within those gates and towers.
> Do my bidding now, I pray,
> Hear me, magic, and obey.

[*There is a flash, and they all start violently.*]
[*A slight pause.*]

Well, I suppose that was it obeying. That means the castle is there, thirty miles away, among the briars and the beech-trees.

PRINCE. And ... and are you going to drag me there by force?

WIZARD. Oh, no indeed.... I'll send you there by magic. That comes next.

MIKEY. Who's going to look after him, when he gets there, Uncle? I mean, cook his supper, and see that his bed's made, and ... and mend his clothes....

WIZARD. Good Mikey. Thoughtful dragon. He shall have as many servants as he wants. He need only call, and they'll come to him.

MIKEY. Won't he be beastly to them?

WIZARD. They only will be shadows. He can't hurt them. As many shadows as he pleases shall obey his orders. They will bring him food, and drink, and whatever clothes and jewels he may ask for. They will make music for him, and exactly perform his bidding ... save only one thing. He shall have no speech or sight of any other human being until the end of twenty years. I don't want to be hard on you, Prince. If you'd like to say you're sorry, and promise to try and behave yourself, I'll make it five years.

PRINCE. You can make it a hundred. I'm not sorry, and I'll never be sorry, and however long you keep me in the castle, I'll never change.

WIZARD. Have it your own way, you silly boy. Tiresome creature. Now I shall call some of your shadow slaves to carry you over the trees, as swiftly as the wind, and lodge you safely in your great castle.

> Come close, you shadows of the night,
> Made of mists and pale moonlight ;
> If you know what you must do,
> Answer, I command you to.

[*A faint chorus of misty voices drifts across the stage.*]

VOICES. We understand. We understand. We understand.

WIZARD. Good. Then there your master stands,
> Take him gently by the hands,
> Lift him over tree and glade
> To the castle that I made ;
> Keep him safe as safe can be
> Till I come to set him free.

[*The* PRINCE *suddenly tries to shake himself free from unseen hands that cling to him.*]

PRINCE. No ... take them away. ...

WIZARD. You've asked for it.
>   All your duties now you know,
>   Shadows, take the Prince and go.

[*Resisting, the* PRINCE *is drawn away swiftly by the invisible hands of the shadows.* COCKY-OLLY *crows, and the stars on the egg disappear.*]

MIKEY. Oh, Uncle, you are clever.

WIZARD. I didn't know I had it in me. Phew.... [*He wipes his forehead with a large handkerchief.*] I haven't done so much real hard magic for years. It takes it out of you, you know. Let me sit down for a minute. [*He sits down on a log, and sighs, and puffs.*] I hope I've done the right thing.

MIKEY. He'll be awfully cross when you do let him go, after twenty years.

WIZARD. No. He'll be tired of being a beast, all by himself. Oh ... you know, I forgot something.
>   One last magic now, I beg,
>   Listen, Cocky-olly's egg.

[*The egg lights up again.*]

[*Admiringly*]. Isn't it clever?
>   Set—around the castle—fair
>   Woods and garden everywhere;
>   Never-fading, deathless flowers,
>   [*He picks a white rose*]
>   Blossoming through winter hours;
>   So the Prince, because of this,
>   Won't forget what beauty is.

[*The rose flies away in the direction of the castle. The stars on the egg vanish.* COCKY *crows again.*]

There. I'm glad I thought of that. After all, we didn't really get to know the Prince very well. And it's just possible that, in spite of all that wildness and temper, he may have liked beautiful things. If he didn't see anything beautiful for twenty years he might forget what it was like, and not know the difference between ugliness and beauty. Then he might never know how to stop being a beast. Now come along in, the bread-and-milk must be really chilly by now. [*He gets up, and puts the egg back into* COCKY's *nest.*] There, Cocky-olly, there's your clever egg. You're a very good boy, and now you can have it back again.

MIKEY. He'll eat it.

WIZARD. Well, it's his egg. Don't be so selfish. [*He takes* MIKEY *by the hand, and starts to go up the path.*] I mustn't forget when the twenty years is up, you know. That would never do. My goodness gracious heavens, that would be a disaster! If I left the Prince there alone too long why—anything might happen to him.

MIKEY. I'll remind you, Uncle.

WIZARD. Oh, child, you've got a memory like a sieve. What shall I do to remind myself? I know. Look, you see this little baby tree? Well, I'll make a mark on it with my penknife...here...like this. In twenty years that mark will have risen, as the tree grows, and it will be...let me see now...just about here, on a level with the top of your head. We'll watch the mark on the tree, and when it's just *there*, we'll go and let the Prince free among men again, and he'll have stopped being a beast. Come along, Mikey.

MIKEY. Yes, Uncle. I'm hungry, aren't you? Good night, Cocky-olly.

WIZARD. I'm starving. Good night, dear Cocky-olly.

[COCKY-OLLY *crows. The* WIZARD *and* MIKEY *start to go up the path to the cottage.*]

And then there's the Prince's horse to think about. I hope he'll get on well with the unicorns.

> [*They go into the cottage, and light streams out over the garden. Then they shut the door.* COCKY-OLLY *crows again.*]

CURTAIN

Act One   *Scene Two*

THE SAME BY DAYLIGHT
Five Hundred Years Later

The only difference in the scene, apart from the daylight, is the fact that the little tree on which the WIZARD *made a mark is now so huge that its top is far out of sight.*

The WIZARD *is sitting downstage, darning his socks with a large needle, and quite unsuitable wool. He has changed his head-gear, and now wears a small skull-cap. Humming happily to himself, he looks up, and beams round him through his square spectacles.*

WIZARD. What a nice day it is, my goodness. [*He bends to his darning again, and sings a little song.*]

> The sunflowers are fizzing,
> The daisies are whizzing,
> The bees are all zizzing
> As they fly along;

[21]

The birds are so funny,
And oh . . . there's a bunny!
The sun is so sunny
I must sing a song;
Tra la, and tra la,
How happy and sunny we are,
Tra la.

[COCKY-OLLY *crows sleepily from his nest.*]

Yes, yes, you sing too, Cocky-olly. It's such a pretty day. And my nephew Mikey is coming to tea, and he's going to stay with us for a whole week. It's some time since I last saw him, he must be getting quite a big dragon by now, you know. But of course, it takes thousands of years for a dragon to grow up, really. He's still quite little. Gracious goodness, it seems only the other day that he was a tiny baby hardly bigger than a newt . . . and that must have been . . . let me see . . . nearly two thousand years ago. Two thousand years. . . . I'm getting on, aren't I. Dear me, how time goes by, it doesn't seem more than a day or two ago.

[*A* VOICE *calls from the direction of the cottage. A man's voice, gentle and courteous.*]

VOICE [*offstage*]. Is there anyone at home?

WIZARD. Now goodness gracious heavens, who's that!

[*He takes off his glasses, and folds up his darning.*]

VOICE [*offstage*]. Hallo, is anyone there?

WIZARD. Yes, my goodness me . . . yes, indeed. I'm here. Come this way, sir.

[*Enter* MR. CLEMENT, *a wealthy and middle-aged merchant. He wears the travelling clothes of a gentleman of 1840. His face is kind and good. He takes off his top-hat, and bows.*]

MR. CLEMENT. Good afternoon, sir.

WIZARD. [*raising his skull-cap*]. And the same to you, sir. It really is, isn't it? A good afternoon, I mean.
MR. CLEMENT. I agree. And what a nice garden you have, right in the middle of the forest. Oh, forgive me.... I forgot to introduce myself. My name is Mr. Clement. I'm a merchant.
WIZARD. My name's Hodge, and you'd hardly credit it if I told you what I am.
MR. CLEMENT. Whatever your calling, sir, you are an excellent gardener.
WIZARD. Oh, middling ... middling. I do my best, Mr. Clement. It's very kind of you ... most flattering ... there are few visitors here, I assure you. I see no one from one century to the next, bar my little nephew and an occasional ... well, some rather odd people who live round here. Won't you sit down?
MR. CLEMENT [*sitting on log*]. Mr. Hodge, you would have no visitor in me, but for the tiresome fact that I tried a short cut through your forest, and lost my way. I should never have ridden off the main road ... never.
WIZARD. Dear, dear, lost your way! How very irritating for you, and you in a hurry no doubt.
MR. CLEMENT. In a great hurry, yes, Mr. Hodge. I've been away from home for a month, trading, you know, and my daughters will be impatient for my return.
WIZARD. How very pleasant to have daughters, pretty things.
MR. CLEMENT. And though I may be speaking who shouldn't, they *are* very pretty, all three of them.
WIZARD. Three? How nice. And their names?
MR. CLEMENT. Jessamine, Jonquiline, and Jane.
WIZARD. Jane must be the youngest, for she has the littlest name.

MR. CLEMENT. Yes, she's the youngest, and the others are just a little bit prettier than she is, but, my dear Mr. Hodge, Jane is so sweet that we have another name for her. We call her Beauty.

WIZARD. Bless her.

MR. CLEMENT. We all do. She has been our blessing, and our mother since my wife died. Jessamine and Jonquiline are very helpless, and, truth to tell, a rather feckless pair. They would be quite lost without Beauty to keep them in order, and run our home for us.

WIZARD. I understand your haste to return to your three dears.

MR. CLEMENT. I have presents for them all. I always take them home the gifts they ask for . . . so that the prospect may comfort them for my absence a little. They are all very young, and dearly love a present.

WIZARD [*eagerly*]. I share their excitement. What are you bringing them this time?

MR. CLEMENT. A gilt mirror for Jessamine, in which she can look at her shining eyes. A carved ivory brush for Jonquiline, with which she can brush her shining hair, and a white rose for Beauty, as sweet as herself.

WIZARD. Just a rose?

MR. CLEMENT. It was her choice. But, look you, my dear sir. I have a little gold necklace for her, as well.

[*They both laugh happily, and the Merchant rises.*]

WIZARD. Yes, yes, you must be on your way. I will show you the path out of the forest that leads to the main road into the country. And, oh, take three red roses from my best bush there . . . one for each of your pretty daughters.

MR. CLEMENT. I thank you for them, sir, but I can't drop you curtseys as they would. You must just *imagine* them for yourself.

> [*They walk up the path towards the cottage.*]

WIZARD. I shall sit here all the afternoon, imagining them.

> [*As they go out of sight round the corner of the cottage* MIKEY *comes in from among the trees. He is picking some leaves off his head and shoulders. He looks the same for all the centuries that have passed, except that his tail may be a fraction longer, though this is hard to tell, and he has a tiny spiky pair of wings on his shoulders. He peers up the path after the* WIZARD *and* MR. CLEMENT.]

MIKEY. That's right, Uncle Hodge, that's the quickest way out of the forest. He'll soon be home again. Good afternoon, Cocky-olly. Good old Cocky-olly! Hallo, Uncle Hodge! I'm here!

> [*The* WIZARD *has come in sight again, and now walks down the path to* MIKEY.]

WIZARD. Hallo, Mikey. How are you? My, you're getting to be quite a big dragon. Another thousand years, and we'll hardly know you. How's your mother?

MIKEY. Very well, thank you, Uncle. She sent you her love, and a basket of strawberries.

WIZARD. Oh, my goodness, how kind of her. How many have you eaten on the way?

MIKEY. Well, I didn't....

WIZARD. Careful, Mikey.

MIKEY. I didn't eat them all.

WIZARD. No, I see that, child. We'll have the last two now, shall we? One for you, and one for me. There.

MIKEY [*placatingly*]. It's such a long way to walk, Uncle Hodge, and I got so hot.

WIZARD. You should have flown, Mikey. What do you think your wings are for?

MIKEY. Oooooh.... I can't... not quite yet....

WIZARD. Now come, come, you mustn't be a cowardly dragon. My goodness me, you could easily fly if you really tried... just short distances at first.... I've known dragons who flew when their wings were much smaller than yours.

MIKEY. I *have* tried.

WIZARD. But not very hard. Your mother told me all about it. I want you to practise a bit, while you're staying here, and when you go home you may be able to say that you've really started to fly. Now you will be a good little dragon, won't you, and have a shot at it? I'd be so proud of you.

MIKEY. I'll do my best, Uncle Hodge.

WIZARD. That's my brave child.

MIKEY [*changing the subject*]. I'd like to see the Merchant's daughters, wouldn't you, Uncle? Beauty sounds a darling.

WIZARD [*shocked*]. Mikey! Were you *listening*? Oh, you naughty dragon. Impolite, and badly-behaved nephew.

MIKEY. Couldn't help it.

WIZARD. Where were you? I didn't see you.

MIKEY. I was up in that tree.

WIZARD. How in the name of goodness did you get up there?

MIKEY. Climbed. Up the other side, while you were darning your socks.

WIZARD. My gracious! Inexplicable and irresponsible creature. Why?

MIKEY. I thought I might ... sort of spread my wings ... and kind of glide down ... and surprise you, Uncle.

WIZARD. Surprise! I'd have jumped out of my skin. And why didn't you?

> [MIKEY *mumbles something.*]

I beg your pardon?

> [MIKEY *mumbles again.*]

And again?

MIKEY. Got a splinter in my finger.

> [*There is a distant, rather creaky, crash and the storm-cone goes jerkily and rustily up its wire to the top of the chimney.*]

WIZARD. Oh, Mikey, you've told a whacker.

> [*An awful silence.*]

You haven't done that for a hundred years. I did think you'd stopped telling whackers altogether.

MIKEY. I'm sorry, Uncle Hodge.

WIZARD. And so am I. Dear, dear me, I never thought I'd see that lie-detector go up again. I hoped it was out of date now. You haven't told a whacker for so long ... why, see how rusty and old it's got. It's five hundred years since I invented that ... almost to the very day.

MIKEY. Five hundred years?

WIZARD. Yes, indeed. You came to stay with me, and I put the lie-warning there, to help you to remember about telling whackers ... don't you remember?

MIKEY. No, Uncle.

WIZARD. You've a memory like a sieve, child. Never mind, it was a very long time ago. This great tree, that you were climbing in, was a little sapling, smaller than

yourself. There was something about it . . . something
odd . . . but I can't for the life of me think what it was.
It couldn't have been very important.

MIKEY. It's a nice tree to climb, Uncle. I was right up
there in the top fork. And I found a funny mark on
the trunk.

WIZARD. What sort of mark, child?

MIKEY. A deep mark . . . like . . . like . . . as though it
was carved in the bark.

WIZARD. Dear me, how very odd. I wonder what it
was. There really is something lurking at the back of
my mind in connection with that tree. Something
about a cutting on the bark . . . dear, dear, and my,
my, what funny things come into one's mind on a hot
summer afternoon. It can't have been anything really
important, or I should remember.

MIKEY. Have you never forgotten anything important,
Uncle?

WIZARD. My memory is not like yours, Mikey. Never
in my life have I failed to remember something really
important.

> [*There is a horrid crash on the gong, and several cones
> go agedly up the wire to the chimney. There is an
> agitated pause.*]

WIZARD. Oh.

> [*Another pause.*]

MIKEY. Never mind, Uncle.

WIZARD. Oh. Oh, Mikey.

MIKEY. Whackers do slip out sometimes, Uncle.

WIZARD. Oh, Mikey . . . it isn't that. Oh, my dear
goodness gracious . . . oh, my kind heaven, what have
I done?

> [*He sits down, and puts his head in his hands.*]

MIKEY. Uncle.... you mustn't take it to heart so. A whacker is only a whacker....

WIZARD. It isn't the whacker, Mikey, it's what I've just remembered. The thing I had forgotten... the mark on the tree... the young sapling... the Beast.

MIKEY. What beast?

WIZARD. I'll never forgive myself. Oh, Mikey, do you not remember at all the young Prince who came here, lost in the forest, and was so bad and wild that I put a spell on him, and shut him in a magic castle, all by himself....

MIKEY. Yes.... yes, Uncle, I remember. For twenty years.

WIZARD. Oh, my hat and my heart! I shut him up alone for five hundred years.

MIKEY [*after a pause*]. Oh dear.

WIZARD. What will have become of him? We must go at once, and find him. He was only a mortal young man, but I put him in the charge of magic, and he will not have aged or died, but he will still be there... alone... and what he will be like after all this time, who can possibly tell. Come along, Mikey. I know a very good little spell that will take us there... it isn't very far.

MIKEY. What do you think he will say to us, Uncle?

WIZARD. Be brave now, Mikey. Be a big dragon. He shall not hurt you, anyway. The fault is all mine. Oh dear, oh dear, what have I done! Put this little charm round your neck, and he can't possibly hurt you.

MIKEY. What about you, Uncle?

WIZARD. Whatever he does to me, I've asked for it. But don't worry, I've got a little charm round my neck, too. I invented them to keep off the mosquitoes. We shall be quite safe. Now hold my hand, and I'll say my spell, and we'll be at the castle in no time at all.

MIKEY. I'm a bit frightened, Uncle.

[*He crosses to the* WIZARD, *and takes his hand.*]

WIZARD. So am I. Not of what may be in store for us, oh indeed no. I'm afraid of what we may find when we get to the castle. What may have happened to that wild young Prince. I put him there to stop him being beastly, and twenty years ... with my magic ... would have cured him. But, in five hundred years, anything may have happened. During that long enchantment ... that terrible injustice ... he may have learned some magic of his own. Oh, Mikey, he may have learned to use magic too strong for me to contest ... oh, these charms are all right ... most efficacious ... but the Prince ... in five hundred years ... hold tight, Mikey, I'm going to say the spell.

MIKEY. Ooooh....

WIZARD. Little spells and minor charms,
        Keep us from all hurts and harms;
        Under the clouds and over the trees,
        Take us to the castle, please.

MIKEY. What do you think we'll find there, Uncle?

WIZARD. Oh, Mikey, in five hundred years the Prince may really have turned into a beast. Here we go ... hold on....

CURTAIN

Act One   *Scene Three*

THE MAGIC CASTLE OF THE BEAST

Here is a turret room, half circular in shape. The roof is arched, and there are pillars here and there, in the dim light, and odd recesses with odder shadows in them. A door at the back is half masked with tapestry. A great window, right, is half-choked by a white rose that has climbed to the window-sill, and even entered the room. Down left, in a niche, stands a beautiful white statue of Eros, holding a broken bow. There is a golden bowl at his feet, full of white roses. The furniture in the room is sparse, and very lovely. There is a table to the left, set with gold dishes, curious flagons, and tall wine cups.

There is no one on the stage, but after a moment the hangings by the door stir, and then a lamp lights up above the Eros.

Then another upstage . . . and another. The tapestries move again, as the BEAST *enters.*

His hair is still tawny, but it is a tawny ruff round his face and head, and his face is that of an alert, young, tawny cat, with shining eyes, and little pointed teeth. He moves swiftly, with arrogant lifted head, and the grace of a cat. He is very like this animal in other ways ; he has the charm, and the unreliable temper, and the pride. His clothes are torn, and his paws are those of the clawed beast. In fact, in five hundred years, the PRINCE *has become a* BEAST *in reality. He is very beautiful, though, if you like that sort of thing.*

He carries a wild duck in his paws, and after a swift move across the room, he throws it on the table, and sprawls into a great chair, to bury his teeth in the feathers, some of which flutter to the ground. Then he looks up quickly, and tightens his paws on the bird . . . as the flagon tilts, of its own accord apparently, over his wine cup. When the flagon sinks back, the BEAST *watches the tapestries stir, and the door open, and close again. Then he takes the cup, and laps the wine, with cat-gulps. The roses by the window are stirring in the wind, and he sees them, puts down the cup, and goes to pat at the roses with his paws. He sniffs at the wind, and pulls a rose, coming downstage to rub it across his cheek, and smells it. He likes the roses.*

He crosses to the statue, and touches it with one paw. He moves away again, smelling his rose. Then he stops and looks defiantly at the statue. The BEAST *has forgotten that he was ever a* PRINCE, *but there is something about the statue and the roses that puzzles him sometimes with a nostalgia which he cannot understand. This annoys him. He shows his annoyance with things just as he did when he was a* PRINCE, *by shouting and threatening, but underneath he is still unhappy, though he himself is not conscious of the fact. Now, still staring*

[32]

at the Eros, he proceeds to tear his rose to shreds. Then he whimpers in sudden reaction, and stoops to pick up the petals. He says to the statue, with a challenge in his voice:

BEAST. Why did you not stop me! [*pause.*] Why do you never answer when I speak to you? Why does no one answer! If I call for music, it comes to me out of nothingness and silence... yet, if I speak, there is nothing *but* silence. Silence... and shadows! And one white statue, that never looks at me. And the white roses, that cannot answer me. [*He beats at the roses in the bowl with his paw, and then looks up at the statue. Its indifference annoys him.*] I would break you, too, if I could, but you are made of marble too hard for me to destroy. All I could break was the bow that you are holding. I can tear my roses to shreds, but there are always roses there to replace them... I've tried to tear them up by the roots, but they grow again. I've hidden you where I shall not see you, but the shadows replace you on your pedestal. [*He stops being malicious, and stares at the statue for a moment, his head on one side.*] You're trying to remind me of something ... I know that. You, with your cold, stone smoothness... and the roses, with their softness, and their scent. What are you trying to tell me? [*He waits almost hopefully, then puts his paws to his head, with the irritation of bewilderment.*] What do you want of me? I'm only an animal, how can I understand you? [*He stops again, and goes closer to the statue, staring at it, and speaks slowly, as though it were prompting him in some strange way.*] You want me to... remember something... something that I... that I have lost... but I cannot remember! I cannot, cannot remember! [*He turns away, angrily.*] I am only a beast, nothing else. I cannot remember ever being anything else . . . [*He has moved away, and now sits in his great chair at the table while he speaks.*] I never shall be anything else ! Leave me alone !

> [*He buries his face in the bird's feathers again, to escape from the influence of the statue. At this moment, the* WIZARD *and* MIKEY *arrive on the windowsill. They look back and down, and* MIKEY *squeaks.*]

MIKEY. It's a long way down, Uncle.

WIZARD. We're at the top of one of the great towers. Don't look down. Be brave. [*He parts the roses, and looks into the room.*] Ssh . . . Mikey . . . .

MIKEY. Ooooooh. . . .

WIZARD. It's the Prince. See his tawny hair. Come on, Mikey. And remember, he can't hurt us. Dear, dear, what shall I say to him, after all this time.

> [*He cautiously approaches the* BEAST, *wondering what to say, with* MIKEY *well behind, and clinging to his hand.*]

WIZARD. Er . . . good afternoon.

> [*The* BEAST *raises his head, and the* WIZARD *recoils. He is stricken with horror and remorse at the sight of his face. The* BEAST *stares at him.*]

WIZARD. Oh !

BEAST. Who are you ?

WIZARD. Don't you remember ?

BEAST [*Glancing at Eros*]. Remember . . . ? [*Back to* WIZARD.] What should I remember ?

WIZARD. We've met before, you know. My goodness, yes! Quite a long time ago, but we *have* met.

BEAST. I've long wanted someone to speak to me, but now I only want to kill ! [*He crouches in his chair to spring.*]

WIZARD. You mustn't do that ! Indeed, you can't. I . . .

the fact is, I've got a sort of charm. Now, please don't get angry, and work yourself up. I've come to apologize for what I've done to you.

BEAST. Ah... [*He lifts his paws to his head, staring at the* WIZARD.] In the forest... you had... a talking lizard....

MIKEY. A dragon!

WIZARD. Sssh!

BEAST. Something happened to me... in the forest... a long time ago.

WIZARD. Er, yes... it was rather a long time. Five hundred years, to be exact.

BEAST. What happened to me?

WIZARD. It's rather awful, but... you see, I shut you up here for twenty years... to stop you being... well, rough is the only word for it. And I... I forgot all about you. And, well... that was five hundred years ago! I do apologize. It's all my fault. I'm terribly sorry. I'll do all I can to help you, Prince.

BEAST [*Lifting his head in his old arrogant way, with a half-memory stirring*]. Prince?

WIZARD. Have you forgotten that you're a Prince?

BEAST. I am nothing but an animal.

WIZARD. No, indeed, you're a Prince.

BEAST. Why do you stand there and mock me? Why do you say things that mean nothing to me? I am an animal.

WIZARD. Oh, Prince....

BEAST [*Rising in a menacing fury*]. Don't dare to call me that! *I am the Beast*. That's the only name I have. [*He advances on the* WIZARD, *with curving claws.*]

MIKEY. Let's go now, Uncle.

WIZARD. Prince... no, I'll call you Beast if you insist.

... Beast, you can't hurt us ... it's my spell, you know. Do sit down, and ... and listen to reason.

> [*The* BEAST *stands over him for a moment, but there is some magic that prevents him being able to touch the* WIZARD *with his savage paws, so he turns away with a snarl, and goes to the window, where he swings round.*]

BEAST. What can I do against magic!

MIKEY. You could shut up, and listen to Uncle.

WIZARD. Mikey! Manners.

BEAST. Well?

WIZARD. Somehow I've got to stop you being a Beast, and get you back into being a Prince again. It's all my fault ... oh, dear ... I must help you.

BEAST. I tell you I have never been anything but what I am. I've never been a Prince.

MIKEY. Well, it's time you started.

BEAST. You! [*He makes a sudden spring, but recoils from the magic. He snarls furiously.*]

MIKEY. I've got that spell, you see. You can't hurt me. Uncle Hodge invented it. It lasts for three months.

BEAST. Does it? [*Cunningly to* WIZARD.] You say you must help me?

WIZARD. Yes, yes, oh indeed, yes. If there's anything I can do to help you, in any way ... all my fault ... if I could only think of some magic that would help you to get back....

BEAST. If there was something that I wanted ... badly....

WIZARD. I swear that I'll get you whatever you want, I'll get it for you, Prince ... I mean, Beast ... whatever the price, I brought you to this, and I must try to get you out of it. Oh, my poor creature, I'll do anything for you....

BEAST. You've sworn it!

WIZARD. Now, don't sound so fierce about it. Yes, I've sworn. Tell me what you want most.

BEAST. Something here in my castle that can answer me when I speak to it. As white and smooth as that statue, but not cold like the marble. As soft and sweet as my roses, that can break as easily in my claws. Something that can speak. Something that can die....

MIKEY. Don't let him, Uncle.

BEAST. You've sworn. And that lizard shall stay here with me. In three months, he will have no magic to protect him, and I shall kill him, unless you fulfil your promise, and bring me what I want.

WIZARD. Oh, my great goodness, what shall I do?

BEAST. Go. Go away, as you came. Let your magic carry you down from the window of my tower. Find me the thing I've asked for.

WIZARD. Oh, Mikey, I'm most terribly sorry, but I promised. Oh dear! You really will have to stay here for a little while.

MIKEY. Oh, Uncle...!

WIZARD. I'll think of some way out, Mikey, I promise you.

MIKEY. You won't forget, will you, Uncle? Three months isn't very long, you know.

WIZARD. I'll never forget anything again, after this. Don't be afraid if you can help it.

MIKEY. I'll try, but... I'll try.

WIZARD. Noble little dragon. Oh, oh, I must think of something, I must! [*He climbs on to the window ledge, and recoils from the height.*] Dear me, it is so high! I hope my spells are in good repair.

BEAST. Go quickly! Bring me back the thing I want.

The living beauty of the roses, the speaking beauty of the statue. I cannot be here *alone* in the silence any longer. I must have something alive . . . that I can kill, if it puzzles me too deeply.

> [*He throws himself into his chair, and buries his face in the bird's feathers again. The* WIZARD *looks puzzled, then he strikes his hand against his brow.*]

WIZARD. Beauty! My goodness, that's an idea! Little Jane, whose other name is Beauty. I think she might know how to deal with him. Mr. Clement said she kept them all in order. Well, [*glancing at the* BEAST] he certainly needs keeping in order. Yes, indeed, my gracious and my magic, he's asked me to bring Beauty here. I think he'll get something he hasn't bargained for!

> [*He waves his hand round and round, clutches his nose, and jumps backwards out of the window, in a loud rushing of wind.* MIKEY, *seeing his Uncle go, gives a little whimper, and the* BEAST *lifts his head swiftly. He looks at* MIKEY. MIKEY *whimpers again, and the* BEAST *snarls at him.*

MIKEY [*quickly*]. I've got another three months!

> [*The* BEAST *snarls again, and drops his head to go on eating the bird.* MIKEY *watches him, with growing fascination.*]

CURTAIN

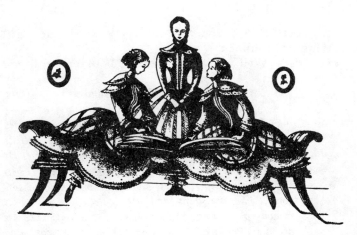

Act Two   *Scene One*

A ROOM IN MR. CLEMENT'S HOUSE

The room is early-Victorian, with red plush curtains, and bobble fringes, draped mantel-shelf, and an elaborate clock imprisoned in a glass case. The table has a bobbled cover, and on it stands a lighted lamp. The fire throws a red glow over the realistic domesticity of the scene, for it is all as cosy and far-removed from magic forests and castles as can be realized. It is a November evening.

All that can be seen of JONQUILINE *and* JESSAMINE *is two frilly behinds, as the sisters crouch before the fire, their noses almost touching the fender.*

JONQUILINE. I don't believe they're going to burst at all. Either of them.

JESSAMINE. Oh, but it said they would, indeed it did. It said so in the book.

JONQUILINE. Are you sure we've done all the right things, Jessamine?

JESSAMINE. Well we can look in the book again, if you like.

> [*So they rise a little, and turn round.* JESSAMINE *picks up a large book from the arm-chair, and they consult it very earnestly. Now that they can be seen properly, they are both very pretty indeed, if a little rumpled from sitting so close to the fire. They wear frilly dresses, with little flat slippers, and pantalettes. Their golden hair is in ringlets, and they have tiny gold earrings. They are twins, and just eighteen, but not a very grown-up eighteen.* JESSAMINE *and* JONQUILINE *are a romantic pair, but they are also very cosy and domestic, like their surroundings. They are like two white Persian kittens, and adorably silly. If there is any perceptible difference of intellect between them,* JESSAMINE *is—by that fraction only—the more sensible of the two.*]

JESSAMINE. There you are, Jonquiline, read it for yourself

JONQUILINE [*reading*]. 'Take as many large chestnuts as there are girls, and place them in a row upon the top fire-bar. Then close your eyes tightly, and recite the following lines. . . .' We did all this, Jessamine.

JESSAMINE. Did we say the lines correctly?

JONQUILINE. I think so. [*She reads aloud.*]

> 'Pretty chestnuts in a row,
> Tell us when our hearts will go;
> She whose chosen nut shall burst
> Is the one will marry first.'

We said all that.

JESSAMINE. Did you shut your eyes? Quite tightly?

JONQUILINE [*shocked*]. Of course.

JESSAMINE. Well, we've waited for ages, and the chestnuts haven't burst.

JONQUILINE. Jessamine... perhaps that means neither of us will get married... ever.

JESSAMINE. Jonquiline....

> [*At this awful thought, their mouths go down, and their pocket-handkerchiefs emerge from their pockets. A little sniff escapes them both.*]

JONQUILINE. How terrible.

> [*They quite break down. At this critical moment of emergency, the door opens, and* JANE *enters, whose other name is* BEAUTY. *She carries candles, and brings the extra light into the scene with her. She is not quite so pretty as her elder sisters, but there is no doubt of her greater sense. A quiet girl, with the serene face of a young Madonna, her calm maternal gentleness throws a soothing veil over most alarms. Her own anxieties, or sorrows, will never be allowed to show. Her hair is parted smoothly, and fastened in a snood. Her dress is less frilly, and she wears a small apron. She is seventeen, but a rather grown-up seventeen. Her sisters amuse and charm her, and she never loses her dignity or sense of humour under the most trying circumstances.*]

BEAUTY. Whatever is the matter now?

JONQUILINE. Oh, Beauty... it is so terrible....

JESSAMINE. We're the most unhappy creatures alive.

BEAUTY [*sensibly*]. Why?

JONQUILINE. You tell her, Jessamine. I... I cannot say it.

JESSAMINE. I don't quite know if I can.

BEAUTY. I think you'd better try.

> [*So they take her hands, and, with little sniffs, explain.*]

JESSAMINE. We took a chestnut each. . . .
JONQUILINE. And said the spell. . . .
JESSAMINE. Out of the book. . . .
   [*They show her the book.*]
   And nothing happened. The chestnuts did *not* burst.
JONQUILINE. So we shall never, never, never get married at all.
JESSAMINE. Oh, Beauty dear, what shall we do?
BEAUTY. I should just stop crying, and being silly, if I were you.
JESSAMINE. Oh, now you're cross with us.
BEAUTY. Indeed I'm not. But why do you worry about a ridiculous book like that? And spells? And nonsense about magic, and chestnuts. You know there's no such thing as magic.
JONQUILINE. Oh, Beauty! No such thing as magic? What about Merlin . . . and the Pied Piper . . . and St. George and the Dragon. . . .
BEAUTY. Those all happened a long time ago. There isn't *any* magic nowadays.
JESSAMINE. Why not?
BEAUTY. Well, it's like . . . like chariots. The Romans had chariots, hundreds of years ago, but there aren't any now. We have carriages, and trains.
JONQUILINE. There's no fun, any more. How dull life is these days.
BEAUTY. Oh, you two are much too romantic. You only think about magic and knights in armour, and great big castles . . . all fairy-tales.
JONQUILINE. Don't you like fairy-tales, Beauty?
BEAUTY. My dear, although I am a whole year younger than you and Jessamine, I have much too much to do to worry my head about nonsense.

JESSAMINE. I suppose we *are* very silly, although we're both eighteen. But oh dear, life was much more fun hundreds of years ago.

BEAUTY. You don't know that, you only think so. Put some more coal on the fire, Jonquiline . . . no, don't . . . you'll only spill it, or dirty your dress. I'll do it. It's very cold outside. I think it may start snowing very early this year.

JONQUILINE. Poor Papa, I hope he is somewhere nice and warm.

JESSAMINE. Perhaps he isn't. Perhaps he's out in the snow.

JONQUILINE. Lost.

JESSAMINE. Miles from anywhere.

JONQUILINE. Cold and hungry.

JESSAMINE. Thinking of his three little daughters.

JONQUILINE. And here we are, all warm and cosy by the fire, while poor Papa. . . .

JESSAMINE. Poor, poor Papa. . . .

BEAUTY. What can be the matter now? [*She seizes their handkerchiefs, and wipes their woeful eyes.*] It isn't even snowing. I only said it might. And Papa is quite old enough to look after himself, even if it did. He'll be home again soon. I know just where he is tonight.

JESSAMINE.
JONQUILINE. } Where?

BEAUTY. At that pretty little inn he told us about. It's called 'The Sleepy Bear', and it is right in the middle of a small country town on the edge of a big forest.

[*She is sitting by the fire, and now starts some sewing. The girls sit at her feet.*]

JESSAMINE. How do you know he is there to-night?

BEAUTY. I know the day when he started back from the

seaport, and he told me just where he would stay each night on his journey home. And he has never come home later than he said he would, except that once—last time—he got lost in the big forest. Don't you remember? He told us about the nice old man he met there. And he brought us a red rose each that the old man sent to us.

JONQUILINE. Perhaps he's got lost again.

JESSAMINE. And perhaps the old man wasn't really a gardener at all, but a wizard.

JONQUILINE. Oh. Suppose he was. Papa said his name was Mr. Hodge.

JESSAMINE. Even a wizard must have a name.

JONQUILINE. I wish we could meet him, and that he really was a wizard.

BEAUTY. My dears, it is just as likely that you will ever meet him as that he really is a wizard.

> [*The windows open at the back of the stage, the lights dim in the room, and there is the* WIZARD. *The* TWINS *scream, but* BEAUTY *rises.*]

WIZARD. Please excuse me. . . .

BEAUTY. Who are you? What do you want?

WIZARD. I'm a friend of your father's. May I come in? My name is Hodge.

JONQUILINE. The wizard!

BEAUTY. Don't be silly, Jonquiline! Please come in, Mr. Hodge.

> [BEAUTY *steps forward and politely helps the* WIZARD *to climb through the window.*]

WIZARD. Thank you, my dear. Thank you. I think you must be Jane, who is called Beauty.

BEAUTY [*curtseying*]. Yes, sir.

WIZARD. And there are Jonquiline and Jessamine.

JONQUILINE
JESSAMINE } [*curtseying*]. Yes, sir.

BEAUTY. Thank you for the roses you sent us, Mr. Hodge.

JESSAMINE.
JONQUILINE. } Thank you very much.

WIZARD. You dear children.

BEAUTY. Come to the fire, sir. You must be cold. Let me take your cloak.

WIZARD. No, no, child. I am in a great hurry. That's why I came to the window, instead of wasting time. In a great hurry... my goodness, yes. Is Mr. Clement at home?

BEAUTY. No, sir. He has been away on business again. But he is on his way back. He will be home next week.

WIZARD. Oh my goodness! next week, I've spent such a long time trying to find his home... nearly three months... *nearly three months*... I haven't got very much longer.

BEAUTY. I don't understand you, Mr. Hodge.

WIZARD. I meant to speak to your father, but I see I must speak to you. Beauty dear, will you come away with me? Now?

BEAUTY. I? Where to, sir?

WIZARD. To a... to a friend of mine. He... er... he's very ill. Quite unlike himself... my goodness, yes! And he needs help, oh, so badly. Dear Beauty, you can help him. Please come with me, and help me to make him better again. Will you?

JONQUILINE. And leave us?

JESSAMINE. All alone?

JONQUILINE. What should we do without you, Beauty?

JESSAMINE. You mustn't go, and leave us all alone.

WIZARD. Beauty... please. It means life or death to my little nephew, and all the world to... that other.
JONQUILINE. But who will wake us up in the morning?
JESSAMINE. And kiss us good night?
JONQUILINE. And run the house?
JESSAMINE. And feed the cat?
JONQUILINE. You can't go away and leave us, Beauty.
JESSAMINE. And what would father say?
WIZARD. What does Beauty say?
BEAUTY [*after a brief pause*]. You must ask Papa.
WIZARD. Where is he?
JESSAMINE. At an inn called 'The Sleepy Bear'.
JONQUILINE. In a little town by the edge of a great forest.
JESSAMINE. But he will never let you take Beauty away from us. Never!
JONQUILINE. We need her. We want her here.

> [*They hold* BEAUTY, *but her troubled eyes are on the* WIZARD.]

JESSAMINE. We want her much more than the presents he is bringing us.
JONQUILINE. More than the gold locket he is bringing for me.
JESSAMINE. More than the pearl ring he is bringing for me.
WIZARD. What is he bringing for Beauty?
JESSAMINE. } A rose.
JONQUILINE. }
WIZARD. At the end of November? Where will he find a rose in the winter?
JESSAMINE. Oh, he will bring her something else instead.
JONQUILINE. He always brings her something lovely, although she asks only for a rose. He loves her, sir, as we all do, and he'll never let her leave us.

JESSAMINE. Never. So it's no use asking him.

WIZARD. I wonder. I know where he can find a rose. Perhaps he may have to let Beauty go.

JESSAMINE. Oh no, indeed he will not think of it!

WIZARD. He may *have* to think of it. My goodness, yes! I must go, my dears. 'The Sleepy Bear', in the village by the forest? I think I can get there before midnight. Good-bye. I must fly! Good-bye. [*He goes to the windows, and they open. Then he waves his hand, and is gone into the dark. The windows close.*]

JESSAMINE. Jonquiline... I think he *was* a wizard.

JONQUILINE. So do I.

JESSAMINE. Beauty... you mustn't let him magic you into going away from us.

JONQUILINE. Oh, you mustn't!

BEAUTY. He said it was life or death .... and all the world.

JESSAMINE. Whatever he said, you cannot go.

[*The clock begins to strike nine.*]

BEAUTY. It's time for bed.

JESSAMINE. Yes, Beauty. Come along, Jonquiline. It's all right, you know. She would never leave us.

BEAUTY. I'll come and kiss you good night.

[*The* TWINS *kiss her, and run out hand in hand.* BEAUTY *goes and takes a chestnut absently from the table, and kneels to put it on the fire-bar.*]

But I may *have* to leave. [*She shuts her eyes, and sings very softly, to the tune of 'Twinkle, twinkle, little star'.*]

'Pretty chestnuts in a row,
  Tell me when my heart will go
  If my chosen nut shall burst
  I'm the one will marry first.'

[49]

[*She opens her eyes.*] There's no such thing as magic. How silly I am. Oh dear . . . 'All the world to . . . that other. . . .' [*There is a small bursting sound from the fireplace.*] Oh . . . mine has burst. How quickly, and how strange.

CURTAIN

Act Two *Scene Two*

THE GATE OF THE BEAST'S CASTLE

The gate is of black iron set in a stone archway. From either side of the arch, tall stone walls hide all except the tops of the trees outside. Through the gate can be seen the density of the forest itself.

There are white roses growing on the walls, and a bush of white roses farther downstage. But the forest trees are bare, and a wind is blowing, as cold as the threatening snow. And snow is lodged in the crevices of the stone wall, and on the gate.

After a moment MIKEY *comes in sight. But it is a very different* MIKEY. *He comes stalking in, his fangs bared in what he considers a very fierce snarl. He has mud on his face and paws, and looks very disreputable. He straightens himself, and sniffs the air, then he snarls and makes a sudden pounce on a dead leaf. He worries it with horrid noises. Then he listens. He snarls, and slinks away off.*

The WIZARD *appears outside the gate. He looks in, and turns to speak over his shoulder.*

WIZARD. Here is the place. And there are the roses, just as I said they would be, blooming in the wind and the snow.

[MR. CLEMENT *comes to the* WIZARD'S *side.*]

MR. CLEMENT. Are you sure it would not be stealing to take one, my dear Mr. Hodge. I wouldn't like to think of stealing.

WIZARD. No, no, my goodness me, it isn't stealing. I ... well, I sort of grew these roses myself. Yes, I really did.

MR. CLEMENT. Amazing. I congratulate you.

WIZARD. Not at all. I rather wish I hadn't now.

MR. CLEMENT. But the gates are locked. And I don't see a bell to ring for the servants.

WIZARD. You wouldn't see the servants if you did. No, no, it's quite all right. The locks will open easily ... it's a ... a ... sort of trick. I'll say a little rhyme, just for luck, you know ... silly of me, isn't it? Then you'll see the locks will open.

MR. CLEMENT. You really astonish me, sir. Most interesting.

WIZARD [*in a hurried gabble*].

> Bolts and staples, locks and bars,
> Under sun, or moon, or stars,
> Iron, or steel, or gold, or brass,
> Move aside and let me pass.

Silly, isn't it? [*He smirks self-consciously at* MR. CLEMENT, *who recoils as the bars slide apart, and the gates open before them.*] But useful. Yes, my goodness! [*He enters the castle garden, looks round him, and sees* MIKEY *lurking in the shadow. He whispers.*] Hallo, Mikey ... get out of sight, do. And what *have* you been doing, you disreputable little dragon?

> [MIKEY *snarls, and retreats backwards. The* WIZARD *stares after him in dismay.*]

MR. CLEMENT. May I come in, Mr. Hodge?

WIZARD. Pardon? Oh, yes, yes, do come in, my goodness. . . .

> [MR. CLEMENT *comes down to his side, and looks round him with wonder.*]

MR. CLEMENT. What a very surprising place. Like a picture out of a fairy-tale. These amazing flowers in the snow, and those great turrets of a dark castle. My two eldest daughters would give anything to be here.

WIZARD. But not your youngest?

MR. CLEMENT. My dear Mr. Hodge, I am most grieved to refuse you anything, but I am afraid nothing would ever persuade Beauty to leave her home, her sisters, and myself. As I told you, I am most deeply sorry to hear about your sick friend, and if anyone could nurse him back to health, it would be Beauty. But there, I would never ask her to do anything that was against her will, and I know that her will is set on staying at home, and looking after us all.

WIZARD. Perhaps we could persuade her to change her mind.

MR. CLEMENT. I do not believe so, Mr. Hodge.

WIZARD. Well, well, we'll see. There are the roses, sir.

MR. CLEMENT. I would not dream of taking one, if it might be missed by its owner. After all, my promise of a rose to Beauty is something of a little game between us. I know she will not be expecting one, at this time of the year.

WIZARD. The more reason for surprising her, then.

MR. CLEMENT. Yes, you are right. Dear little Beauty, how very nice to surprise her so. [*He puts out his hand and plucks a white rose. The wind rises to a dreadful howl, there is a terrifying screaming snarl from offstage, and the next moment the* BEAST *comes swiftly from the shadows, and stands facing the two men with his paws held menacingly before him.*]

BEAST. Who has robbed me? Which of you has robbed me?

WIZARD. Oh ... er ... neither of us ... now please do be calm.

BEAST. Someone has stolen a rose from me.... I felt the branch break, here in my heart. Who has taken my rose?

MR. CLEMENT. Who ... what ... are you?

BEAST. You're the one. You've robbed me. I'll have your life in exchange. [*He prepares to spring, but the* WIZARD *comes down to his side.*]

WIZARD. No, no, just a minute. Please don't be so hasty. Just listen to me, like a nice good ... Beast.

MR. CLEMENT. Mr. Hodge ... you said it wasn't stealing....

WIZARD. Nor it is. Just let me speak to him. Go and stand by the gate. Just for a moment. [*He holds the* BEAST *by the sleeve, but the* BEAST *throws him off.*] Oh my goodness, don't be so rough!

BEAST. If it were not for your magic, you would die now, you old fool. But *he* has no magic, and he has stolen my rose.

WIZARD. I gave you the roses, remember.

BEAST. Five hundred years ago you gave them to me. They are mine, now, and no one has a right to take them away.

WIZARD. Well, never mind about that. . . .

BEAST. I'll kill him for it! My roses . . . my roses. . . .

WIZARD. Oh, do listen. You can get something in exchange more valuable to you than his life.

BEAST. I only want his life.

WIZARD. No. There was something you wanted more than anything in the world. Living, speaking Beauty, here in your castle. He can bring it to you.

BEAST. He? That thief?

WIZARD. Ahem . . . Mr. Clement, yes. You must ask him. Tell him . . . er . . . tell him he must bring Beauty here in exchange for the rose. Just for a short visit, you understand. Say, for a week, perhaps. Tell him how your health has . . . er, suffered . . . and how it will benefit from a short stay by Beauty. Say I'll be here to keep an eye on her, as well. Why, you might ask him to bring Jonquiline and Jessamine and we could all have a lovely time. . . .

BEAST. Be quiet.

WIZARD. What?

BEAST. I want no advice from you. Get out of my way.

WIZARD. Oh, I say now . . . my gracious. . . .

    [*But the* BEAST *elbows him aside and advances on the horrified* MR. CLEMENT.]

BEAST. Listen to me, you robber.

MR. CLEMENT. Mr. Hodge. . . .

WIZARD. I can't stop him. . . .

BEAST. You've stolen my rose, and you should die for it.

MR. CLEMENT. I had no intention of stealing, I promise you.
BEAST. Yet you stole.
MR. CLEMENT. Just a rose.
BEAST. Yet one of the only things I have in the world to love. Your life would be a small repayment for it. For all that, you may go without hurt. . . .
MR. CLEMENT. I'm most grateful, sir.
WIZARD. Oh, so am I.
BEAST. On a condition, robber. That you bring Beauty here to take your place.
MR. CLEMENT. To take my place?
BEAST. Bring Beauty to my castle.
WIZARD. Oh, now please . . . no. . . .
MR. CLEMENT. I absolutely refuse. I shall not dream of doing any such thing. It's unheard of. You're a savage, sir! I would certainly die, before I brought Beauty within a mile of you, or your castle.
BEAST. You have no choice, robber. You hold my rose in your hands. It is not a common rose, but magic. And by that magic you are bound, whether you choose or no, to return here within two days. If you come yourself, you die. If Beauty comes in your place, you are free to live as long as you please.
MR. CLEMENT. I'll not let Beauty come here to die!
BEAST. That is for you to decide, within two days. Take this ring. It, also, is magic. Put it on your hand, if you decide to return, and it will bring you here on the wind. Or let Beauty wear it, and the wind will bring Beauty to my castle.
MR. CLEMENT. I'll not even go. You may kill me now, if kill you must.

BEAST. You are bound by magic. Go, take your horse and ride away. In two days you must return, or send Beauty in your place. Go.

MR. CLEMENT. Mr. Hodge. . . .

WIZARD. I'm most awfully sorry, but I don't know what to do.

MR. CLEMENT. Mr. Hodge. . . .

> [*But the gates have opened, and the wind rises to a howl, and* MR. CLEMENT *is swept, resisting, out into the forest. The gates close.*]

WIZARD. You really mustn't do these things. It's . . . it's awful of you. I can't believe you mean half you say, but it sounds quite terrible.

BEAST. I mean all I say, and more.

WIZARD. If Beauty comes here, you couldn't behave cruelly.

BEAST. I can kill.

WIZARD. I forbid it. I absolutely will not have it.

BEAST. You will leave my castle. And not come back. Go out of those gates, and never let me see you again.

WIZARD. No. No. Oh dear, this is all going wrong! I asked Mr. Clement here, and offered him a rose because I thought you might persuade him to bring Beauty in exchange, just for a little visit. I never meant this sort of dreadful goings-on to happen.

BEAST. Go.

> [*The wind rises again, the gates open, and the* WIZARD *is swept protesting through them.*]

WIZARD. You can't do this sort of thing! It's . . . it's most wicked of you. No . . . let me explain . . . do listen to reason. Don't be so naughty. . . . [*But the gates have closed and he is outside. He clutches at the bars.*] Please let me in. Beast ... you mustn't hurt Beauty. You mustn't! Listen to me.

BEAST. I put a command on the gates not to open again for anyone except the robber returning to die, or for Beauty. [*He picks a rose, and places it in the centre of the gates. He laughs, and stalks away into the shadows.*]

WIZARD [*beating on the gates*]. Come back ... Beast, come back.

[MIKEY *comes sniffing in and raises himself to peer at the* WIZARD.]

WIZARD. Mikey ... Mikey ... you must help me.

MIKEY. Hallo, Uncle. Look, I'm a beast too. [*He pounces on something, and worries it, snarling.*]

WIZARD. Mikey, what has happened to you? You've got to listen to me. Stop that awful noise, and listen! Mikey, you mustn't let the Beast hurt Beauty. Do you hear me?

MIKEY. I like the Beast. I like doing the things that he does. I like pouncing on things, and tearing them to bits. I like eating chickens with their feathers on. I like snarling ... and biting ... and growling ... when I grow up I'm not going to be a Dragon, I'm going to be a Beast, too.

WIZARD. No ... no! You must be a Dragon, and fly. ...

MIKEY. I like crawling, and getting muddy best. And if the Beast wants to hurt Beauty, whatever that may be, I'll help him to do it, and I'll be a Beast too. [*He snarls and pounces off. The* WIZARD *groans and beats on the gates.*]

WIZARD. Mikey! Mikey! Naughty, bad dragon ... come back ... oh my goodness, what a dreadful mess I've made of everything. What shall I do? First the Beast, and now Mikey ... and next ... oh dear, what will I do if anything happens to Beauty?

    [*But only the wind answers him, and he shakes the gates unavailingly.*]

CURTAIN

Act Two *Scene Three*

THE ROOM IN MR. CLEMENT'S HOUSE

MR. CLEMENT *sits in the armchair by the fire, his head in his hands. At his feet sit* JESSAMINE *and* JONQUILINE, *in the last stages of sobbing despair.* BEAUTY *stands, centre, with the white rose in her hand. Her face is sad, and calm.*

BEAUTY. Of course I must go, father. There's no question about it.
JESSAMINE. No, we won't let you.
JONQUILINE. How can we?
BEAUTY. Would you prefer that Father should go?
JESSAMINE. We don't want anyone to.
JONQUILINE. Not Papa, or you.
BEAUTY. Silly things . . . no one's going to die. The poor

creature had just lost his temper because Papa took his rose. He . . . he didn't intend any of the horrid things he said. No one talks like that, these days. . . .

JESSAMINE. But, Beauty . . . this is magic.

BEAUTY. Nonsense.

JONQUILINE. It can't be nonsense if Papa says it, and he told us it was magic.

BEAUTY. Poor Papa is very tired, and worried. He didn't mean. . . .

MR. CLEMENT. Beauty dear, it *is* magic. If you had seen that . . . that strange creature, and heard his voice. . . .

BEAUTY. The thought of him frightens me . . . terribly . . . but I'm so sorry, too. How dreadful to look like that. How dreadful for a man to look like a beast.

MR. CLEMENT. It might be a beast that looks like a man.

[BEAUTY *shakes her head and raises the rose to her cheek.*]

BEAUTY. He loved the rose, Papa. He is a man. Poor thing.

JESSAMINE. Never mind what he is, Beauty. You shan't go near the horrid creature.

BEAUTY. I must.

JESSAMINE. I don't think I like magic as much as I did.

MR. CLEMENT. And it is magic, as strong and strange as any you've read about in fairy-tales. Would I have said a word of all this to you? Would I have come back here, and reported his threats? Would I have let you know the dreadful fact that I must go back to that dark castle to die?

JONQUILINE. Papa!

MR. CLEMENT. If I was not wearing this ring I would have said no word of anything. I would have kissed you all, and gone away back to the Beast. I am heartbroken that I've been forced to speak like this, but the ring compelled me. See, I cannot even tear it off my finger. It clings like a live thing.

BEAUTY. Give it to me, Papa.

MR. CLEMENT. No, child. Once and for all, I am going back myself. Not you.

BEAUTY. But he wanted me. He asked for me.

MR. CLEMENT. And threatened you with death, when you should come.

BEAUTY. Only threatened, Papa. He promised death to you. Oh, please believe me, he couldn't mean any of it. He is ill . . . mad . . . angry . . . but he wouldn't kill me. I can look after myself.

MR. CLEMENT. You haven't seen him.

BEAUTY. But I intend to. Now, Papa, my mind is made up. You are very tired after your journey, and you talk of magic . . . and . . . and things like that. But I do not mean to be afraid of anything I have not seen for myself. I shall go now, and put on my coat and bonnet. Then you shall tell me how to get to this strange house in the wood, and the time that the trains go. You must give me the ring to wear, since he seems to want me to wear it . . . and then you shall take me to visit him.

MR. CLEMENT. Child, you make it all sound so simple. You have no idea what you are doing. I shall not allow you to go.

BEAUTY. Nevertheless, I am going to put on my bonnet.
 [*She touches her cheek again with the rose, and goes quietly out of the room. The* TWINS *breaks into a fresh outburst of tears.*]

MR. CLEMENT [*calling*]. Beauty, come back, child! Oh, but she shall not go.

JESSAMINE. Oh, Papa. . . .

JONQUILINE. Papa. . . .
JESSAMINE. What shall we do, Papa?
JONQUILINE. We shall die without her, Papa.
MR. CLEMENT. She will not be going away, Jonquiline.
JESSAMINE. But she's so strong-minded, Papa.
MR. CLEMENT. I will not allow her to go.
JESSAMINE. Who will kiss us good night?
JONQUILINE. Who will remember to feed the canary?
JESSAMINE. Who will remind us of our dancing lessons?
MR. CLEMENT. Beauty will do all these things. She is staying here, I assure you.
JESSAMINE. How can we make her stay?
JONQUILINE. If only we could go instead, Jessamine.
JESSAMINE. Oh, if only we could.
MR. CLEMENT. You silly girls. You know you wouldn't go.
JONQUILINE. Wouldn't we, Papa?
JESSAMINE. No, perhaps we wouldn't.
JONQUILINE. Oh dear, how silly we are. We ought to be brave, and go.
JESSAMINE. But we wouldn't know what to do when we got there.
JONQUILINE. We'd be so frightened.
JESSAMINE. We'd scream if we saw the Beast.
JONQUILINE. And die if he spoke to us.
JESSAMINE. Oh, his sharp teeth!
JONQUILINE. Oh, his savage claws!
JESSAMINE. Papa! Don't let him come near us!
MR. CLEMENT. Hush, children. None of you will ever see him.

> [*Enter* BEAUTY. *She wears her best bonnet and jacket, and carries a little reticule in one gloved hand. In the other she holds the rose.*]

BEAUTY. I am ready, Papa. When do the trains go?

MR. CLEMENT. Oh, my darling child, you still will not understand. There is no train, no timetable, no ordinary facts. The creature lives in a magic castle in an enchanted forest. If you wear this ring, you will be carried there on the wings of the night-wind. And never be seen again.

BEAUTY. You are dreaming, dear Papa. There is no such thing as a magic ring, and an enchanted castle, and wizards.

JESSAMINE. But there is. We saw one.

JONQUILINE. She means a wizard.

JESSAMINE. You know we did, Beauty. When the window flew open. . . .

JONQUILINE. By magic.

JESSAMINE. And the wizard stood there, in his flowing cloak.

BEAUTY. That was Mr. Hodge, the gardener.

JESSAMINE. The wizard.

MR. CLEMENT. I have an idea that you may be right.

BEAUTY. Nonsense, my dears. You're all too romantic. If we ever see Mr. Hodge again I shall ask him if he's a wizard, just to hear him laugh at you all.

[*The windows open very slowly, and there is* HODGE, *very small and depressed, and huddled in his cloak. The* TWINS *give a squeal of fright.*]

WIZARD. I never felt less like laughing in all my life.

BEAUTY. Mr. Hodge. . . .

WIZARD. Yes, my dear. Mr. Hodge, the gardener, and . . . oh dear me . . . such a silly old wizard.

JESSAMINE. You see? I told you.

BEAUTY. I think you're all being very odd.

MR. CLEMENT. Mr. Hodge, whatever you are, please

bear me out in this . . . my daughter must not go to the Beast's castle.

WIZARD. I don't know what to say for the best.

MR. CLEMENT. I must go back. He . . . he really can't mean to kill me.

WIZARD. All the same, I'm very much afraid he does.

JESSAMINE. No, Papa!

JONQUILINE. Oh, oh. . . . Papa. . . .

MR. CLEMENT. It is like some dreadful nightmare. I cannot believe such things can happen nowadays.

WIZARD. Anything can happen when you start messing about with magic. It's all my fault, my goodness, yes. I'm so terribly sorry.

BEAUTY. Poor Mr. Hodge. But I'm sure everything will be all right, really. Come along, Papa, I'm ready to go.

JESSAMINE. Beauty!

JONQUILINE. Oh, oh . . . Beauty. . . .

MR. CLEMENT. You are not going, Beauty.

WIZARD. You don't know what a terrible decision you're making, child. You don't know the Beast.

BEAUTY. Do you? Do any of you know the Beast? [*She crosses to her father and takes his hand.*] Give me the ring, Papa.

MR. CLEMENT. I can't take it off my finger.

BEAUTY. I can, Papa. [*She takes the ring from his hand, and slides it on to her own gloved finger.*] Look.

[*The lights dim down in the room. The windows open, and the moonlight brightens.*]

WIZARD. Oh, you shouldn't go. I came to warn you!

MR. CLEMENT. You're not to go, child.

JESSAMINE. Beauty. . . .

JONQUILINE. Beauty . . . don't leave us!

BEAUTY. Oh . . . oh . . . what is lifting me? What is

drawing me away ... to the window ... to the wind in the night. ...

    [*She moves slowly along the shaft of light that falls from the window through the darkened room.*]

JESSAMINE. Come back, Beauty!
JONQUILINE. We need you.
WIZARD. Don't let her go!
MR. CLEMENT. Beauty, come back, we need you.
JESSAMINE. Beauty, we need you!
JONQUILINE. We need you!
BEAUTY. I'm needed elsewhere.

[*She has drifted across the room, and lightly up on to the window-ledge. Now she lifts the rose to her cheek, holds her ringed hand out in front of her, and disappears into the darkness.*]

CURTAIN

Act Two   *Scene Four*

THE ENTRANCE TO THE BEAST'S CASTLE

An arched stone doorway, with a door of iron-hinged oak. At either side stretch the stone walls of the castle, and a flight of stone steps leads up to the closed door. Roses are growing on the walls, and on the balustrades of the steps. Snow lies thickly on the steps themselves.

    The BEAST *is standing on the steps, with a rose in his paws. He sniffs the air.* MIKEY *comes stalking in from downstage with a dead bird in his mouth. He looks more disreputable than ever.*

BEAST. What have you there, lizard? [MIKEY *snarls at him.*] Answer, when I speak to you! I know you have

a tongue. You spoke often enough when first you
came here. It was strange to hear anyone talk...
and good. Now, you seem to have lost your voice, and
be as silent as the stone... except for your snarling!
[*He moves down to* MIKEY, *who snarls at him again.*] Why
have you forgotten to speak, lizard? [*He snatches away
the bird.*] Answer me, I tell you.

> [MIKEY *snaps at the bird, and the* BEAST *dangles it
> annoyingly above his head, so that he has to jump up
> and makes useless snatches at it. The* BEAST *laughs.*]

You could not even catch the bird for yourself!
And I have tried to teach you to hunt, during these
three months. You will never make a hunter, clumsy,
noisy lizard.

> [MIKEY *is whining and scrabbling at him. He laughs
> again, and pushes* MIKEY *down into a sprawl on the
> ground at his feet.*]

Oh, you are quite safe, lizard, because of your
magic! It will not help you much longer. [*But he
speaks only teasingly and now he turns away, saying in a
rather surprised voice*] I think I would not even desire to
destroy you, if only you would speak to me. Yes, even
you... you lizard!

> [*He throws the bird back to* MIKEY, *who pounces on
> it and worries it.*]

Do you hate me so much that you will not speak?
Or have you forgotten the way... here, in this silent
castle?

MIKEY [*in a curious grunt*]. I copied you... now I don't
want to speak.

BEAST. Do I speak only in snarling?

> [MIKEY *nods, and starts to eat the bird. The* BEAST
> *goes up the steps again, and picks another rose.*]

Why do you try to imitate me? Because you hate me?

> [MIKEY *looks up and shakes his head vigorously, then drops it again into the feathers.*]

Then I cannot understand. [*He starts to tear the rose, stops suddenly, and stares at the torn petals. He gives a little whimper.*] You should not try to be like me, lizard. I am nothing but destruction.

> [*They both suddenly raise their heads, and sniff at the air. The* BEAST *gives a growl, imitated by* MIKEY *rather squeakily. There is a rushing sound like a high wind.*]

The gates have opened.

> [*He drops the rose, and stands staring offstage.* MIKEY *growls again.*]

Quiet.

> [*A pause.*]

What is that? Mikey... answer me... what is it?

MIKEY [*grunting*]. Girl.

BEAST. What should a girl be doing here?

MIKEY. Dunno.

BEAST. She has no right to be here. [*He raises his paws to his face.*]

MIKEY. I'll frighten her off for you.

BEAST. If she sees me, she will be frightened enough. Oh... she must not see me... I must hide my face and my claws... I am not a sight for any girl to look on.... Let me hide myself. [*He runs up the steps, and the castle doors open. He goes in.*]

> [MIKEY *looks offstage L. for a moment. Then growls, and hides behind the side of the staircase. After a slight pause,* BEAUTY *enters Left. She stares round her,*

nervously, and then smooths her skirt and pats her hair and bonnet into order. She straightens herself bravely, and looks round.]

BEAUTY. The roses need pruning. [*Her voice is a little shaky, but she is trying to be firm. She crosses to the foot of the steps.*] And the steps need cleaning. Dear me, I'm afraid ... the ... the owner has been very neglectful. [*She goes up the steps to the door.*] No bell? No knocker? I cannot shout. [*She looks round the door for a bell-rope. Then she taps rather quietly on the door itself.*] No one could possibly hear that, you silly girl. [*She knocks again, rather louder. A pause.*] It will sound extremely vulgar of me to *bang* on the door, but if people won't have proper knockers.... [*She bangs quite loudly.*]

[*Faint voices answer her from the other side of the door.*]

VOICES. Who is there? Who is there? Who is there?

[BEAUTY *recoils. Then she stiffens herself firmly.*]

BEAUTY. It is I, Jane Clement.

VOICES. That is not the name. Not the name. Not the right name.

BEAUTY. It *is* my right name.

VOICES. Who was knocking on the door? We may only open to one with the right name. What is your right name?

BEAUTY [*hesitantly*]. I am called Beauty.

VOICES. Beauty. She is called Beauty. Let the bell ring. Beauty is here.

BEAUTY. What bell? Do you mean me? There's no bell for me to ring.

VOICES. Yes ... yes ... pull the rose ... pull the stem of the roses.

BEAUTY. The stem of the roses? That's an odd bell-rope. [*She moves her hand to the stem of the creeper beside the door when she catches a glimpse of* MIKEY, *down behind the steps, peering at her interestedly.*]

Who is there?

[MIKEY *growls, and retreats into the shadow. She comes forward on the steps.*]

Are you hiding? Who are you? Oh, is it a dog? A cat? Do come out. It's... it's very lonely here, and rather frightening. I would be glad of company. [*She comes down the steps, and sees* MIKEY.] What... oh dear ... what are you?

[MIKEY *advances, and snarls at her. She gives a little gasp and runs back to the door.*]

Don't... don't be angry with me! Don't growl at me. I've not harmed you. I've come to see you. Is this your castle? Are you... are you the Beast?

MIKEY [*in scorn*]. Me, the Beast? No.

BEAUTY. Oh, you can speak?

MIKEY. I can, but I won't. See! [*He snarls, and makes a little dart at her.*]

BEAUTY. No! Don't be so horrid! Go away. You must not make such dreadful noises. Is this the proper way to greet a guest?

MIKEY. Frightened... you're frightened... grrr!

BEAUTY. Oh, go away. You're a nasty thing. I wish someone would come... even the Beast himself would be nicer than you, you rude little thing.

MIKEY. Ha, ha!

BEAUTY. I'll ring the bell.

[*She pulls at the stem of the rose-creeper, and immediately a bell starts slowly ringing high above their heads. It sounds grim and sinister.* BEAUTY *backs away from* MIKEY *until she is standing against the door.*]

MIKEY. Grrr ... grrr ... you're frightened! I'm frightening you.
BEAUTY. You're horrid. I'll tell him. ... I'll tell the Beast.
MIKEY. Hoo, hoo ... If you're afraid of me, wait till you see the Beast.
BEAUTY. I'm not afraid. I wish he'd come ... now. ... Beast! Beast!
> [*The bell stops ringing suddenly, and the door opens. The* BEAST *is standing in the doorway.* BEAUTY *starts to scream, then checks herself, with a hand over her mouth.*]

BEAST. I tried to hide myself. But you called me. What do you want with me? Why have you come here at all?
BEAUTY. I ... I ... I've come to see you, sir.
BEAST. Then look at me, and go quickly.
BEAUTY. You want me to go?
BEAST. Why should you want to stay? You can see me. [*He spreads out his paws, and she recoils.*] You're safe enough, girl. But go away, quickly.
BEAUTY. I ... I'm not afraid ... not very much afraid. ...
BEAST. I am only a beast. I am not safe company for anyone. Please go away.
BEAUTY. But I thought you were expecting me, sir. I was told ... some voices told me to ring the bell, if my name was the one they expected to hear.
BEAST. What is your name, girl?
BEAUTY. Ja—I am called Beauty, sir. [*She gives him a little curtsey, and holds out her rose, and her gloved hand with the ring on it.*] See. This is your ring, that brought me here. And the white rose from your garden.

BEAST. You are . . . Beauty? You?
BEAUTY. Yes, sir. May I . . . may I come into your castle?
BEAST. You're not afraid?
BEAUTY. I am a little afraid, sir, but I . . . I shall try not to show it to the best of my ability.

> [*He stands aside, and she goes up to the doorway. She recoils a little as she passes him.*]

BEAST. You draw aside from me.
BEAUTY. I beg your pardon. That was silly.
BEAST. You are right to draw aside, Beauty.
BEAUTY. It was ill-mannered of me, sir. May I go in?

> [*The* BEAST *stares at her, then makes a clumsy bow. She glances down at* MIKEY.]

Tell that impolite little animal to wipe his paws before *he* comes in.

> [*The bell starts ringing again, as* BEAUTY *goes into the castle. The* BEAST *stands in the doorway looking after her as she goes out of sight. Then he looks down at his paws. He says to* MIKEY :

BEAST. You heard what she said about your paws.

> [MIKEY *growls and wipes his paws sulkily against his own seat. The* BEAST *brushes his paws against each other, and whimpers softly.*]

CURTAIN

Act Three   *Scene One*

A ROOM IN THE CASTLE
Same as Act 1 Scene 3

The lamps are alight, and BEAUTY *is filling the bowl at the feet of Eros with roses. She crosses to the window to pick one, starts to cross to Eros with it, then turns again and looks out of the window into the darkness.*

BEAUTY. I wish they wouldn't stay out in the dark. I don't know what to do with them. Mikey is quite troublesome enough without any further encouragement. And the Beast gets disturbed so by the moonlight ... as though he had not enough already to disturb his poor mind. Oh, he shouldn't go out in the night! Ah,

well.... [*She sighs, and goes to add her rose to the bowlful.*]
Oh, Eros—I never thought the statue of love could look
so aloof. [*She sighs again.*] How silent it is here. I wish
there wasn't quite so much silence.

> [*A minor chord of music sounds through the room,
> and dies quietly away.*]

Oh! Oh, dear, I cannot become accustomed to this
sort of thing. Now, I mustn't hurt their feelings. [*She
speaks very politely to the air.*] Thank you, I should like
you to play to me, very much.

> [*Another chord sweeps across the room, then a quiet
> and gentle air is heard*].

[*Smiles*]. It's very pretty, however you do it. [*She
crosses to the table, and sets out some dishes.*] I hope they'll
come in to supper. [*She sighs.*] I do wonder how
Jessamine and Jonquiline, and Papa, are managing. I
wonder what they are having for supper now. Not cold
venison, and wine. Oh dear, I would like a rice pudding. And I always hated them so. [*She crosses to sit on
the window-seat.*] Jonquiline, and Jessamine ... and
Papa ... are you thinking about me, sometimes?
Have you forgotten me? [*She takes out a handkerchief, and
dabs her nose.*] Now don't be silly. I'm being as bad as
the twins. How could they forget me, in one month?
[*She blows her nose firmly, and sniffs a little.*] Besides, I
haven't forgotten them, so why should they forget me?
Don't be silly. You're grown-up now. But oh, Papa ...
Jonquiline ... Jessamine ... I do so miss you. It's
lonely here, with no one to talk to, and no one to hug.
[*Out comes her handkerchief again.*] And oh, are you remembering about the canary? [*She sits sobbing helplessly, and after a moment the door opens.*]

> [*The* BEAST *comes into the room. He looks at her in*

[78]

silence. He puts out a paw towards her, then hesitates. But a louder sob from BEAUTY *brings him to her side. He touches her shoulder.*]

BEAST. Don't... [*As he touches her, she recoils, rising to her feet with a cry.*]

BEAUTY. Oh....

BEAST. Don't run away. I'm not going to hurt you.

BEAUTY. Oh... I'm... I'm sorry. You startled me. I didn't mean to run away.

BEAST. It's stupid of you to show how much you fear me. It makes me angry. And when I'm angry, I am not safe company. You should hide your fear.

BEAUTY. I do try.

BEAST [*turning away*]. Yes. You try hard.

BEAUTY. Don't be angry with me.

BEAST. I am not angry.

BEAUTY. Don't be hurt. I jumped away from you... only because I was startled. I... I'm not nearly so much afraid of you as I used to be.

BEAST. Do you like being here, in my castle?

BEAUTY. Yes... I... yes, I like being here.

BEAST. Why were you crying?

BEAUTY. I was sad.

BEAST. About what?

BEAUTY. Oh, why must you question me!

BEAST. I want to know.

BEAUTY. Please....

BEAST. Tell me why you were crying?

BEAUTY. You must not speak so roughly, Beast. It's... it's most impolite.

BEAST. What else do you expect from a beast? Look at my paws!

BEAUTY. They've never hurt me.

BEAST. But they could. Look at them now, look at the mud on them ... the mud ... and the blood. ...

BEAUTY. You've been hunting, again. Why must you do it? Oh Beast, why must you go out into the darkness to kill? Look at your knees, all torn again and muddy. And the laces all bedraggled on your sleeves. Why are you so wild, and rough? Why cannot you be gentle?

BEAST. You call me by my name. Is a beast gentle?

BEAUTY. Yes, oh yes. Beasts are very gentle. And you're a man, too. Men should be gentle.

BEAST. Oh, leave me alone! [*He brushes her aside, and goes to the window.*]

BEAUTY. Beast ... dear Beast. ...

BEAST. Leave me alone. You must not anger me. You should never come near me when that happens. You should run away and hide.

BEAUTY. You wouldn't hurt me.

BEAST. How do you know what I may do when the darkness closes down on my mind? I cannot tell myself what I shall do. ...

BEAUTY. Why are you trying to frighten me?

BEAST. Why were you crying when I came in? Answer me.

BEAUTY. Oh. ...

BEAST. Answer me! [*He catches her by the wrist, and stares down at her angrily.*]

BEAUTY. Don't. ...

BEAST. You must not anger me, Beauty. I've warned you. Oh, I've warned you.

BEAUTY. You're hurting me.

BEAST. I can see that you're afraid. That's dangerous. You should never let me see that you're afraid. Why were you crying, Beauty?

BEAUTY. You're cruel!

BEAST. Your eyes are like the eyes of a deer. Why were you crying, Beauty?

BEAUTY [*screaming*]. Oh! Let me go!

BEAST. Were you crying because you want to leave me?

BEAUTY. Yes!

BEAST. Because you hate me?

BEAUTY. Yes!

> [*He lets her go so suddenly that she falls on the ground, and lies there sobbing.*]

BEAST. I thought so. [*He paces about the room for a moment. Then stands looking down at* BEAUTY.] Why do you hate me so?

BEAUTY [*through her tears*]. You made me say that. You were horrid. I would never have said it, otherwise.

BEAST. Beauty, do you hate me?

BEAUTY. No ... yes ... sometimes ... I don't know....

> [*The* BEAST *stares down at her for a moment, then stoops and lifts her to her feet. She shakes him off, and sits on the window-seat.*]

BEAST. You want to go away? To leave the castle?

BEAUTY. I want to go home.

BEAST. I need you here, Beauty.

BEAUTY. I miss my father, and my sisters. It's so lonely here.

BEAST. Yes, it's lonely here.

BEAUTY. And it's so silent.

BEAST. So silent.

BEAUTY. There's no one to talk to me.

BEAST. I am here.

BEAUTY. But when you aren't, it's so lonely.

BEAST. I was alone here for five hundred years.

BEAUTY. I am only a girl. I've always been used to my

home, and my sisters, and Papa. You must not expect more of me than I can give.

BEAST. And you want to go?

BEAUTY. Would you let me go?

BEAST. You ask a terrible thing of me. You're the first living creature who has been kind to me, sung to me ... you've made this feel like a home to me ... and you ask me to let you go.

BEAUTY. Please ... please ... I can't bear it here, any more. Please let me go.

BEAST. For ever?

BEAUTY. Do you mean ... that I can go?

BEAST. For ever, Beauty?

BEAUTY. Must I come back?

BEAST. If you do not return, I shall die.

BEAUTY. No!

BEAST. How can I be alone with the roses, and the statue, when Beauty has walked alive through my castle? Without you, I can no longer live.

BEAUTY. What shall I do?

BEAST. If you want to go, I shall not prevent you.

BEAUTY. Oh, dear Beast....

BEAST. But come back to me, Beauty, or I shall die.

BEAUTY. Then ... then I shall come back.

[*The* BEAST *crosses and picks a rose—he takes a ring from his finger.*]

BEAST. Take these. When you put the ring on your finger, it will carry you home on the wind. Take the rose, and keep it carefully. You may stay away for a week, and the rose will bloom without fading. But if you stay away longer than the week I give you ... the rose will wither and die. And as it fades, so shall I fade, and as it dies, so shall I die. You must not stay away for an hour after the rose begins to droop. Put the ring on your hand again, and come back to me. Beauty... you must come back to me again.

[*He kneels beside her, and gives her the rose.*]

BEAUTY. I shall come back.

[*He drops his head on her knee, and she strokes his hair as though he were an animal.*]

I promise to come back, Beast... dear Beast.

[*He kisses her hand, and puts the ring on her finger. She crosses to the window. She steps lightly on to the window-seat.*]

Jonquiline... Jessamine... Papa ... [*She is gone into the darkness.*]

[*The* BEAST *drops his head on his arms, and whimpers.*]

BEAST. Beauty... Beauty... you must come back to me.

CURTAIN

Act Three   *Scene Two*

BEAUTY'S BEDROOM IN HER FATHER'S HOUSE

A small bed, draped with white frills, and a little dressing-table and stool, also frilled. On the table is a silver vase with the white rose in it. Also a ring-holder with the Beast's ring on it.

JESSAMINE and JONQUILINE are sitting side by side on the bed, in frilly white night-dresses, and dressing-gowns. Their hair is pinned up on top of their heads with curl-papers. They look very sad, and sniff occasionally. After a few moments JESSAMINE *rubs her nose with the back of her hand.*

JESSAMINE. If we weren't quite so silly, we could think of the right things to say that would keep her here with us.

JONQUILINE. But we can't. We've said everything we

can think of. We've begged and begged her to stay . . . and oh, how we've cried.

JESSAMINE. She has made up her mind.

JONQUILINE. And she's going to leave us, again.

JESSAMINE. And go back to that horrid Beast, and his great dark castle. She can't like the Beast as much as she likes us.

JONQUILINE. How could she?

JESSAMINE. She's sorry for him. All this week she has been worrying about him . . . and wondering if he is having proper meals, and staying out at night in the forest. She's *very* sorry for him.

JONQUILINE. I'm a bit sorry for him too, but not very much. Not if he takes Beauty away from us.

JESSAMINE. And he is. She's going away.

JONQUILINE. Now.

JESSAMINE. We can't stop her.

JONQUILINE. I hate the Beast!

JESSAMINE. It's not proper to hate, Jonquiline.

JONQUILINE. I don't care. I hate him.

JESSAMINE. So do I.

JONQUILINE. I wish his horrid rose would die! [*She jumps up, and crosses to the rose.*] It smells so sweet. Yet I wish it would die.

JESSAMINE. Then the Beast would die, also.

JONQUILINE. Then . . . then . . . oh dear, I wish we could steal the ring.

JESSAMINE. Then Beauty couldn't go back to him, at all.

JONQUILINE. Shall we steal it? Here it is, Jessamine.
    [*She holds up the ring.*]

JESSAMINE. That would be most improper of us, Jonquiline.

JONQUILINE. It would keep Beauty here with us.

JESSAMINE. And the Beast would die.
JONQUILINE. Do you think he would . . . really?
JESSAMINE. Beauty says he would.
JONQUILINE. Then I suppose we mustn't steal it . . . and Beauty must leave us. For ever . . . [*she sobs*] . . . oh, I do hate the Beast, and his rose, and this ring!
> [*She stamps her foot, and the ring falls and rolls away across the floor.*]

JESSAMINE. Oh, be careful!
JONQUILINE. I don't care! I don't care! I hope it's lost! I want Beauty!
JESSAMINE. But where has it gone? Jonquiline, help me . . . I can't find the ring.
JONQUILINE. I don't ca . . . what did you say?
JESSAMINE. I can*not* find the ring!
JONQUILINE. Oh, my goodness!
> [*They search the floor without success for the ring.*]

JESSAMINE. Oh, be quick! It's nearly ten o'clock.
JONQUILINE. There is no sign of it.
JESSAMINE. Ooh! Oh! Jonquiline . . . it must have gone down the mouse-hole.
JONQUILINE. Oh. Oh dear. Let us look.
> [*They kneel on the floor, and all that can be seen of them are their frilly behinds as they crouch to look down the mouse-hole in the corner.*]

JESSAMINE. I can't see it.
JONQUILINE. It's dark in there.
JESSAMINE. I can't get my hand inside.
JONQUILINE. It's lost.
JESSAMINE. Completely lost.
JONQUILINE. For ever.
JESSAMINE. What shall we say to Beauty?
> [*They both sit bolt upright on their heels.*]

JONQUILINE. Oh, my goodness, what will she say to us?
JESSAMINE. Jonquiline....
JONQUILINE. I cannot tell her. I cannot. She'll say I'm silly.
JESSAMINE. We must make up a story.
JONQUILINE. But what?
JESSAMINE. Don't cry, Jonquiline. If the ring is lost there's no use crying. And Beauty need not know just how silly you ... we ... have been this time.
JONQUILINE. What will you tell her?
JESSAMINE. I shall say ... now listen, Jonquiline ... this is quite clever of me ... I shall say that a big bird flew through the window and carried the ring off the dressing-table, and away out into the night again. A very big bird stole it.
JONQUILINE. But that isn't true.
JESSAMINE. Well ... it's not exactly a lie. It's a sort of excuse.
JONQUILINE. It sounds rather like a lie.
JESSAMINE. Do you want to tell Beauty that you dropped it down a mouse-hole?
JONQUILINE. No. Oh, no.
JESSAMINE. Well, you see, a mouse has really stolen it. If I say it was a bird, instead of a mouse ... well, a bird is only a bigger mouse with wings.
JONQUILINE. It sounds better now that you have explained it.
JESSAMINE. It's just on ten o'clock.
JONQUILINE. And here comes Papa, with Beauty.
JESSAMINE. Now, do be brave, Jonquiline.

[BEAUTY *enters with* MR. CLEMENT. *She is holding his hand, and wears bonnet and jacket, not the ones she wore before, which she has presumably left at the castle.*]

BEAUTY. Not in bed yet, darlings? I went to your room to kiss you, but found you gone.

JESSAMINE. We came here, to your room, Beauty.

BEAUTY. And no slippers on. You'll catch colds, both of you.

JONQUILINE. Oh, Beauty....

JESSAMINE. Dear, dear Beauty....

BEAUTY. Jessamine, Jonquiline... don't cry. I'll come back soon. The Beast will let me come and see you again, very soon. Dry your eyes. Here... here's my handkerchief. Dry your eyes.

[*As they sniff and dry their eyes, a clock strikes ten very slowly.* BEAUTY *speaks on the first stroke.*]

Ten o'clock. I must go.

MR. CLEMENT. Oh, my dear.

BEAUTY. I promised. He will be waiting for me.

JESSAMINE. Beauty....

JONQUILINE. Oh, dear... oh, dear....

BEAUTY. Good-bye Papa. [*She kisses him.*] I will come back soon. Good-bye, my pets....

JESSAMINE. Oh, Beauty... please forgive us.

BEAUTY. Forgive you? For what?

JONQUILINE. We're so silly.

BEAUTY. You're darlings. [*She kisses them.*] Good-bye. Go to bed, quickly, and I'll see you all again soon. [*She looks for the ring.*] Where is the ring?

MR. CLEMENT. What, my dear?

BEAUTY. Where is my ring? It isn't here!

JESSAMINE. It's... it's....

JONQUILINE. Oh, Beauty....

BEAUTY. But it has struck ten. I should be back. Where

is the ring? [*She searches frantically on the dressing-table.*]

JESSAMINE. It's been stolen, Beauty.

BEAUTY. Have you taken it? Oh, give it back to me, my dears.... you must give it back!

JESSAMINE. We can't.

JONQUILINE. We would if we could.

MR. CLEMENT. Have you taken the ring, girls?

BEAUTY. Oh, please.... oh, please ... I'm late already....

JESSAMINE. It was stolen by ... by a bird.

JONQUILINE. A big bird. With wings.

JESSAMINE. It flew through the window.

JONQUILINE. And stole it.

JESSAMINE. And flew away again.

MR. CLEMENT. The window is shut.

JESSAMINE. Oh. Is it?

JONQUILINE. Oh, dear.

JESSAMINE. It ... it must have been magic.

MR. CLEMENT. More magic!

BEAUTY. Then I cannot go back tonight. What shall I do?

JESSAMINE. Stay with us.

JONQUILINE. Forget about the Beast.

BEAUTY. Forget my Beast?

JONQUILINE. We want you more than he does.

JESSAMINE. Much more.

BEAUTY [*Despairingly*]. Please ... please ... go to bed ... leave me alone. I must find my way back to him ... how can I find my way back? To the forest and the castle ... oh, do go to bed, my darlings ... good night ... good night....

JONQUILINE. Yes. Good night, dear Beauty.

JESSAMINE. Good night, Beauty.
> [*They kiss her unresponsive cheeks, and turn to the door.*]

[*As they go.*] We've been more than silly this time, Jonquiline. We've been bad.
JONQUILINE. Oooooooh....
> [*They go out, very depressed.*]

MR. CLEMENT. My dear child, perhaps it is all for the best. It was a most unsuitable situation.
BEAUTY. Oh, Papa, what shall I do?
MR. CLEMENT. I don't approve of all this magic.
BEAUTY. What shall I do?
MR. CLEMENT. Perhaps ... perhaps the bird was all part of the dream. This must all have been a dream really, you know. Now we can wake up.
BEAUTY. My poor Beast.
MR. CLEMENT. Go to sleep, my darling, and when you wake up you'll have forgotten all about the Beast. So shall we all, I hope. This is only a dream. Good night, child.

[*He kisses her, and goes to the door.*]

BEAUTY. Papa....
MR. CLEMENT. Yes, my dear.
BEAUTY. Nothing. Good night, Papa.
MR. CLEMENT. Good night, Beauty. Forget your dream.
> [*He goes out*].

BEAUTY [*Covers her eyes with her hands.*] Was it a dream? Is there no castle? No forest? And no Beast? Have I only dreamed of a creature that was wild and strange and ... loved me?
> [*A chord of music sweeps through the room and the rose in its silver vase droops.*]

Oh ... oh ... [*She runs to the rose, and cups her hands*

protectingly round it.] You must not fade. No, no, you must not droop and die! It's all true. There's no dream. The rose is going to die... and what is happening to the Beast? *My* Beast! You mustn't die, my Beast. How can I make you hear me? How can I find you again?

> [*The music sounds again through the room, very low and melancholy. A petal falls from the rose in* BEAUTY'S *hands.*]

Oh, no, stay alive, my rose! Stay alive, my Beast! My poor Beast... my poor Beast....

CURTAIN

Act Three   *Scene Three*

THE ROOM IN THE BEAST'S CASTLE, THE SAME NIGHT

The lamps are lit, and the table is set with a more civilized meal than those usually indulged in by the BEAST. *There are roses and candles on the table, also glasses and covers.*

> [*The* BEAST *stands staring out of the window. He is quite still. After a moment, a far-off bell rings once.*]

BEAST [*Shouting*]. No! Not yet! It isn't ten yet. [*He turns and paces across the room. Then to the table. He lifts a cover.*] It's getting cold again. [*He goes back to the window.*] It isn't ten yet. Another few minutes.

> [MIKEY *comes in, looking a lot cleaner than when last seen.*]

MIKEY. Isn't she here?

BEAST [*Defiantly*]. It isn't time yet.
MIKEY. It's after ten.
BEAST. No.
MIKEY. The bell has started to strike four times, now, and each time you've stopped it.
BEAST. It cannot be time. She is not here.
> [*The bell rings again. The* BEAST *gives a strange cry.*]
> No. No. Not yet.
MIKEY. It's long after ten. She isn't coming.
BEAST. I'll kill you if you say that.
MIKEY. Oh . . . well, perhaps she's been delayed.
BEAST. She has the ring. What should delay her?
MIKEY. Dunno. I'm hungry. . . .
BEAST. Why doesn't she come?
MIKEY. Could I have something to eat? I've washed my hands three times.
BEAST. It isn't time.
MIKEY. You keep saying that, Beast, and the food has all been heated up twice, and I'm simply starving.
BEAST. Be quiet. Leave me alone. Go away.
MIKEY. But I'm so hungry.
BEAST. There's game in the woods . . . why must you come whining to me, now?
MIKEY. Beauty didn't like us to go eating things raw. You know she didn't.
BEAST. Then be silent.
MIKEY [*pause*]. I've brushed my wings.
BEAST [*Dully*]. What?
MIKEY. I brushed my wings twice, and I put a jug of roses in Beauty's room. Do you think she'll be pleased? That is, if she ever comes back.
> [*The* BEAST *crosses, and seizes him by the neck. But*

his attention is not on MIKEY *and his threats are spoken in anguish, not anger.*]

BEAST. How can you dare to say that ! She promised. It ... it isn't time, yet. ...

[*The bell strikes again and goes on striking.*]

MIKEY. Listen ... let me go.

BEAST. I'll kill you.

MIKEY. Don't ! You're hurting me. Beast !

BEAST. You've no magic now. I can kill you if I choose.

MIKEY. No ! Beast ! Don't ... it's me ... Mikey. ...

BEAST. She'll come back when the bell strikes ten.

MIKEY. It's striking, now.

BEAST. No. [*He releases* MIKEY, *and stands listening. When the bell stops, he goes to the window, and stands staring out. There is a long silence.*] She will not come.

MIKEY. Oh, Beast. ...

BEAST. She never meant to come back.

MIKEY. Beauty wouldn't break her promise for nothing.

BEAST. She never meant to keep it. She hated me ... she feared me. She has escaped from me. [*He drops on to the window-seat, with his head on his arms.*]

MIKEY. Beast. ...

[*But the* BEAST *whimpers, like a heart-stricken animal.* MIKEY *fills a glass with wine, and brings it to him.*]

MIKEY. Would you like this ?

[*But the* BEAST *will not speak. He whimpers again.*]

Wouldn't you like some food? I'm awfully hungry.

BEAST. Ah. ...

[*The* BEAST *rises and goes swiftly to the table where he lifts the roses and dashes them on the ground. He sweeps the table clear with his paws, and leans against the tapestries on the wall, gasping helplessly, and tearing open the neck of his tunic.*]

[MIKEY *watches, awestruck.*]

MIKEY. You have made an awful mess. [*He picks up a roasted chicken-leg, and is about to eat it when he sees the* BEAST *reeling.*] Beast! What's the matter with you? [*But the* BEAST *staggers to a chair, where he crouches sobbing.* MIKEY *goes to him.*] Don't cry. Please don't cry. I don't know what to do. I didn't know you could cry. [*He wipes his own eyes, and nibbles the chicken.*] I'm frightened. Where's Beauty? She ought to be here. She could make him listen. Beast . . . Beast . . . don't cry like that. You'll die. Oh, dear, I wish Uncle was here. [*He looks out of the window, and sniffs loudly. He is still eating the chicken desperately. Calling.*] Uncle! Oh, he can't hear. I don't know any magic to bring him here.

[*The* BEAST *moans, and his hand drops beside him limply.*]

He is going to die. [*He lifts the* BEAST'S *head on to his knee, and sucks the chicken bone frantically.*] What shall I do? What can I do? I've forgotten the only magic I ever knew. Uncle taught me a spell. It would have brought him here like lightning . . . but I can't remember. Dear Beast, don't die!

[*The* BEAST *moans, and opens his eyes.*]

BEAST. Mikey...

MIKEY. Oh Beast, are you all right? Do be all right.

BEAST. No, Mikey. I'm going to die . . . Mikey. . . .

MIKEY. What?

BEAST. Eat your supper. [*His head drops limply again.*]

MIKEY [*sobs*]. Ooooooooh. . . . [*He sucks the chicken-bone again, and looks at it helplessly.*] I might make up a spell. But it wouldn't work for me. I'm not a magician, or anything. [*He sniffs and holds up the bone.*]

All the magic I have known
Please be in this chicken bone;
I don't know a thing about it,
But I cannot do without it.
Magic, magic, magic dear,
Oh, do bring my Uncle here.

It won't, of course.

[*But the* WIZARD *is standing in the window.*]

Uncle Hodge! Oh, Uncle Hodge!

WIZARD. I was blown straight up the chimney.

MIKEY [*Frantic with relief*]. That was me. Uncle....

WIZARD. What's happened?

MIKEY. Look.

WIZARD. The Beast....Oh my good gracious... what's the matter with him?

MIKEY. He let Beauty go home for a week, and she hasn't come back... and he's dying, Uncle.

WIZARD. Oh, Mikey... what can we do?

MIKEY. She must come back. Quickly.

WIZARD. Give him to me, Mikey. Stand up, child. Let me look at him.

[MIKEY *rises and the* WIZARD *sits down holding the* BEAST'S *head on his knee. The* BEAST *whimpers.*]

Beast... do listen to me....

MIKEY. He won't, Uncle.

WIZARD. Poor creature.

MIKEY. Beauty must come back. She said she would come after a week ... and the week was over when the bell struck ten. He tried to stop it striking ... he tried so hard to believe she was coming. But she didn't come.

WIZARD. Poor Beast, poor child.

MIKEY. Why do you call him that?

WIZARD. I've been a very stupid old man, Mikey. I punished him for being rough and angry ... but he was really unhappy. We thought him a beast, but he was a child. I have brought tragedy to him, and he needed love. Poor child.

MIKEY. Bring Beauty back ... she must come back. ...

WIZARD. I have no spell to bring her here again. The ring was her only means of return. I know no other enchantment.

MIKEY. Can we send a message?

    [*The* WIZARD *shakes his head.* MIKEY *sucks his bone frantically.*]

WIZARD. Nothing can bring her here, if she has decided not to come. If she was afraid ... and broke her promise. ...

MIKEY. I ... I ... I could tell her ... that he needs her. ...

WIZARD. You, child? How can you tell her?

MIKEY. You told me where she lives.

WIZARD. But Mikey. ...

    [MIKEY *jumps up on the window-seat and looks down, and out. He recoils from the height.*]

Mikey, be careful. What are you doing? You'll fall.

MIKEY. No ... I must fly ... I've got to fly. ... [*He jumps from the window.*]

WIZARD. Mikey!

CURTAIN

Act Three   *Scene Four*

BEAUTY'S BEDROOM, AGAIN

BEAUTY *is sitting on her bed, her eyes closed. The rose has only one petal left on it, where it lies in her hands. She raises one hand, and wipes the tears from her cheeks. After a moment, the door opens, and* JESSAMINE *and* JONQUILINE *appear, in their night-dresses.*

JESSAMINE [*whispering*]. She's not asleep.
JONQUILINE. She mustn't see us.
BEAUTY [*eyes closed*]. Go back to bed. You can't do anything, darlings.
    [*They run to her, and stand looking at her helplessly.*]
JESSAMINE. Don't cry so, Beauty.
JONQUILINE. It's all our fault.
JESSAMINE. We *are* so sorry.
BEAUTY. How could you help it? Have you got your slippers on?

JESSAMINE. No, Beauty.
JONQUILINE. We forgot.
BEAUTY. You'll get such colds. [*Her eyes are still closed, and she speaks faintly through her tears.*]
JESSAMINE. It isn't cold.
> [*The windows open suddenly, there is a rush of snow, and* MIKEY *lands spread-eagled on the floor. The* TWINS *scream, and jump up on the bed, where they clutch their skirts round their ankles.*]

JONQUILINE. What is it?
JESSAMINE. An alligator!
BEAUTY. Mikey! [*She runs to him.*] Oh . . . Mikey.
JESSAMINE. He'll bite you!
JONQUILINE. Be careful, Beauty!
BEAUTY. Mikey . . . tell me. . . .
MIKEY [*Breathlessly*]. He's going to die . . . you must come . . . you broke your promise. . . .
BEAUTY. No. I lost the ring.
JESSAMINE. Beauty. . . .
JONQUILINE. Beauty, what is it?
JESSAMINE. *Is* it an alligator?
BEAUTY. He's a dragon.
MIKEY [*Proudly*]. And I flew! I can fly miles.
BEAUTY. Can you carry me back to the castle, Mikey?
MIKEY. Oh. Well, I . . . I'm not sure that I can. My wings are dreadful tired.
BEAUTY. I don't know how you managed to fly so far . . . you dear little dragon. [*She kisses him.*]
MIKEY [*bashfully*]. Oh. . . .
BEAUTY. How can I get to him, Mikey?
MIKEY. I thought you'd have the ring.
BEAUTY. Would I break my word?
MIKEY. Well, I thought it was funny.

BEAUTY. Would I let him die? My own Beast?
MIKEY. He thinks you hate him.
BEAUTY. Poor creature....
MIKEY. He's dying because he thinks you hate him.
BEAUTY. If he dies, I have failed him unspeakably. And the ring is lost. Stolen....
JESSAMINE. No... strayed. It strayed, Beauty.
BEAUTY. You told me....
JESSAMINE. It wasn't quite true.
JONQUILINE. Not altogether.
BEAUTY. You said a bird stole it. Where is it?
JESSAMINE. It's... it's....
JONQUILINE. Actually....
JESSAMINE. It's down that mouse-hole.
BEAUTY. Jessamine! Jonquiline!
  [*They hang their heads, and sob a little.*]
MIKEY. Don't cry. A whacker is only a whacker.
BEAUTY. How can we get it out?
MIKEY. I'll try.
JESSAMINE. We couldn't get our hands inside.
JONQUILINE. It's very narrow.
MIKEY. I'll snuffle it out of the hole.
  [*He kneels by the hole, and makes dreadful snuffling noises.*]
BEAUTY. Oh, Mikey, if only you can!
JESSAMINE. He'll choke himself.
JONQUILINE. He's snuffling up a lot of dust.
BEAUTY. Bring me the ring, Mikey. Please.
  [MIKEY *suddenly chokes, and backs to centre, where he sits coughing.*]
JONQUILINE. He's swallowed the mouse!
JESSAMINE. No, the ring.
BEAUTY. Here, Mikey, give it to me. [*She pats him rapidly*

on the back, he chokes, and she takes the ring from his lips.]
Oh, Mikey... you darling... [*She turns on her sisters, smiling through her tears.*] Go back to bed, my dears. You must not get cold. Come along, Mikey... hold my hand... come quickly. There's only one petal left now on the rose.

> [*She puts the ring on her finger and holding* MIKEY'S *hand she runs with him to the window and away.*]

CURTAIN

Act Three *Scene Five*

THE ROOM IN THE BEAST'S CASTLE

The debris has been cleared from the floor and table. A narrow pallet couch has been brought in, covered with a rich velvet drape. On this lies the BEAST, *his face to the tapestries, and his paw hanging limply downstage. The* WIZARD *is filling a glass with wine. He brings it to the* BEAST *and stoops over him.*

WIZARD. Please try to listen to me. What can I do if you won't listen? My goodness, you can't just lie there in silence, and die. You must make some effort. Do try. Drink this, there's a good Beast. Oh, now it's all spilt. You're not trying at all. You've just given up. That's very naughty of you. Oh dear.... [*He puts the glass back on the table, and goes to the window.*] If anything's happened to Mikey I shall never forgive myself. This will be a lesson to me not to interfere with people's lives, till I know more about them. That poor boy, there. He had no one to care about him, so he was hurt and wild ... and I tried to punish him for it, instead of helping him. I did it for the best ... but, oh my good gracious, look what's happened. And Beauty ... whatever has happened to Beauty? ... She has been frightened, maybe hurt, too ... and whatever shall I say to Mikey's mother? [*He takes the* BEAST'S *limp paw in his hands.*] What can I say to *you*? How can I tell you how sorry I am? I dabbled in magic, but my magic is no help now. I know nothing that will bring you back to life again. I think only one person in the world can do that. And she will not come. How cold you are. [*He covers the* BEAST *more closely, and lifts his paw on to the bed. He crosses to look at the statue on its pedestal.*] Can't you help him, Eros? He loved you ... but you're only stone. And the roses? He loved those, too. But nothing loves him strongly enough to be able to save him now.

> [*There is a rush of wind, and* BEAUTY *stands in the window.* MIKEY *crouches beside her.*]

BEAUTY. Beast! Beast!
WIZARD. Oh....
BEAUTY. Where is my Beast?
> [*The* WIZARD *gestures towards the bed, and* BEAUTY *speeds across the room to kneel beside it.*]

My dear....
MIKEY. I flew, Uncle.
WIZARD. Hush.
BEAUTY. Wake up. Turn round, my Beast. I'm back.

I've come back. I didn't break my word. I always meant to come back to you.

> [*But the* BEAST *does not move. She turns to the* WIZARD.]

Is he dead?

WIZARD. Very nearly, Beauty.

BEAUTY. I'll not let him die. He shan't. Beast.... Beast... turn your head, and look at me. You must! Listen, I'm talking to you. It's Beauty....

WIZARD. You can't make him hear you.

BEAUTY. I will. Beast, you mustn't die. [*She holds his paw against her cheek, and kisses its fur.*]

[*The* BEAST *stirs, and whimpers.*]

MIKEY. Oh, Beauty....

BEAUTY. Dear Beast, my dear Beast.... I'll never go away from you again, if you'll listen to me. I was silly to be frightened of you. What does it matter about your hands, and your face... you're my Beast... I love you.

BEAST. Beauty....

BEAUTY. Yes. Yes. I'm here. Turn your head, and look.

BEAST. Don't call me back to life... I don't want to live ... you must let me die....

BEAUTY. You're not to.

BEAST. I must.

BEAUTY. I won't have it! [*She rises to her feet, and stiffens firmly.*] Enough of this nonsense. Stand up. You know you can. You're not to lie there, and let yourself die.... I'll not allow it.

MIKEY. Don't be nasty to him... he's not....

WIZARD. Hush, Mikey. She knows better than we do.

BEAUTY. Beast... Beast... stand up.

BEAST. No.

[104]

BEAUTY. You must stand up—you're not a beast. You're a Prince.

WIZARD. Oh, you clever girl!

BEAUTY. Prince . . . Prince . . . why are you lying there, as though you were a beast? Stand up, *Prince.*

> [*The* BEAST *turns his head, but his face is that of the* PRINCE. *He looks at* BEAUTY, *and raises his hands to shield his face. He stares at his hands from which the paw-gloves have slid away.*]

Oh.

> [*The* PRINCE *looks at her again, and rises unsteadily to his feet. He holds out one hand gropingly.*]

PRINCE [*in a low, uncertain voice*]. Beauty?

> [*He goes a little towards her. She recoils slightly.*]

BEAUTY. Where is my Beast?

> [*He drops on his knees at her feet, and hides his head in her skirt. He whimpers.*]

Oh, my poor creature. [*She strokes his hair, as though he were an animal.*]

> [*The* WIZARD *goes to* MIKEY *by the window.*]

WIZARD. My brave and noble dragon.

MIKEY. I flew—

WIZARD. Mikey—I've just remembered a most useful bit of magic.

MIKEY. What, Uncle?

> *The* WIZARD *waves his hands, and after a second* MR CLEMENT *appears at the window, with* JESSAMINE *and* JONQUILINE *holding his hands. He wears a dressing-gown, and they their night-dresses.*]

WIZARD. Good evening, Mr. Clement.

MR. CLEMENT. Good evening, Mr. Hodge. I am having a very odd dream.

WIZARD. Are you enjoying it?

MR. CLEMENT. Very much indeed, so far. I hope it goes on for a long time.

WIZARD. It will, Mr. Clement.

BEAUTY. Have you got your slippers on?

JESSAMINE.
JONQUILINE. } Er ... yes, Beauty....

> [*In the distance can be heard a creaky crash on a gong, as thirty miles away, the lie-detector cone goes up the wire.*]

MIKEY. What a whacker!

WIZARD. Dear me, I shall have to oil that lie-detector—it may be needed again.

JESSAMINE. What a beautiful place!

JONQUILINE. What a beautiful place!

JESSAMINE. Can we live here for ever, Beauty?

JONQUILINE. May we, Papa?

MR. CLEMENT. It would be very pleasant, my dears.

BEAUTY. May we live here for ever, dear Prince?

> [*The PRINCE raises his head, still with great uncertainty. He is not at all sure who he is, or who these strangers are, but he trusts Beauty.*]

PRINCE. Why yes ... of course ... Beauty.

> [*She puts her head back on his shoulder, and smiles up at him, then she puts out one hand and touches the statue above them.*]

BEAUTY. Look at Eros. I always thought he looked so distant, but I never noticed he was smiling like that.

PRINCE. And still will not look at us.

> [BEAUTY *merely moves down to face upstage to the statue, and leads the* PRINCE *with her.*]

BEAUTY. He is looking now.

> [*While they stand together, in a dream, at the feet of*

> *Eros, her head again on the Prince's shoulder, the* WIZARD *takes a deep and happy breath, and goes into action.*]

WIZARD. I shall put the greatest spell I know all round the forest, so that no one shall ever stray here by accident. Only those who really need magic shall find it. The forest will be invisible to any others. Yet we will still be living here, you in your castle ... I in my cottage....

BEAUTY [*still in her dream*]. And what about the servants?

WIZARD [*startled*]. What did you say, my dear?

BEAUTY [*without turning*]. I cannot have all these shadows. It's most unnerving.

WIZARD. I shall call on my neighbour to-morrow ... a most reliable witch. She had a lot of people who had been transformed at one time or another, and she sent them all into service here. She can turn them all back into people again, and fill your castle with living men and women. Servants, and courtiers, and friends.

JONQUILINE. Jessamine!

JESSAMINE. Jonquiline!

WIZARD. Yes, and you may marry, after all.

JESSAMINE [*shyly*]. I forgot you were a wizard.

WIZARD. This is a fairy-tale, so we can all live happily ever after.

> [BEAUTY *gives the* PRINCE *a very gentle push, and he takes a deep breath and remembers his manners.*]

PRINCE. May I ... give you all my very humble thanks ... and a welcome to this castle?

BEAUTY. Oh, you'll make a very good prince, my dear.

> [JESSAMINE *and* JONQUILINE *are beckoned forward by* BEAUTY *to curtsey to the* PRINCE. MR. CLEMENT *leads the* WIZARD *downstage.*]

MR. CLEMENT. Mr. Hodge, something is puzzling me badly.

WIZARD. Dear me, what is it?

MR. CLEMENT. I know I've read this story somewhere ... once upon a time.

MIKEY. Was I in it? Did it say how I flew ... for miles?

MR. CLEMENT. It was called ... yes, I think it was called 'Beauty and the Beast'.

WIZARD. This *is* the story of Beauty and the Beast.

MR. CLEMENT. I don't quite understand.

WIZARD. You mustn't try, Mr. Clement. This is magic.

CURTAIN

THE WIZARD'S SONG

Music by
Ronald S. Hill

The Plotters of Cabbage Patch Corner
Musical Play for Children
DAVID WOOD
6 male, 4 female
Audience participation. One basic setting.

The insects live in a busy world in the garden. Their existence, however, is always overshadowed by the humans—the Big Ones. Infuriated by constant "spraying" the unattractive Slug, Greenfly and Maggot call for rebellion, strikes, ruination of the garden. The others oppose this and war is declared. Fortune swings one way and the other in a series of bitter campaigns. The garden goes to ruin, and the Big Ones decide to build a garage on it. This brings the insects to their senses. They combine to restore the garden to its original beauty and thus preserve their home.

(ROYALTY, $25-$20)

The Ant and the Grasshopper
(Children's Play) Fantasy
ROB DEARBORN
9 characters (1 clearly female, the others can be either male or female)

The classic tale updated with contemporary language and themes understood by today's children—and adults. An uptight, super-industrious ant has just opened a new branch ant-hole when an irresponsible, "hippy-type" grasshopper moves in right next door. Ant resists Grasshopper's offers to join him and his friends, Caterpillar and Ladybug in play—in fact he says play is a bad word. For his diligence Ant is promoted by autocratic, imperious Queen Ant. With his two assistants Ant prepares for the coming winter. Grasshopper, naturally, doesn't believe in winter or any of the gloomy warnings of Ant and even the attacks of hungry Spider fails to daunt his optimism. But winter does come, and both Grasshopper, who has no food or shelter, and Ant, who has no friends and has never had any fun, discover at last that there is more to life than they thought.

(ROYALTY, $15)

CHARACTERS

HODGE, *the wizard*

MIKEY, *his nephew*

THE PRINCE

MR. CLEMENT, *a merchant*

JESSAMINE

JONQUILINE

JANE, *who is called* **BEAUTY**

SETTINGS

ACT ONE

Scene 1   The Wizard's Back Garden
Scene 2   The same, 500 years later
Scene 3   A room in the Beast's Castle

ACT TWO

Scene 1   A room in Mr. Clement's House
Scene 2   The Gate of the Beast's Castle
Scene 3   The room in Mr. Clement's House
Scene 4   The Entrance to the Beast's Castle

ACT THREE

Scene 1   The room in the Beast's Castle, a month later
Scene 2   Beauty's bedroom, a week later
Scene 3   The room in the Beast's Castle
Scene 4   Beauty's bedroom
Scene 5   The room in the Beast's Castle

TIME

1340 and 1840